Wedding group: *front row, seated, left to right:* The Earl of Ulster, Lady Davina Windsor, Lady Rose Windsor, Andrew Ferguson, Lady Rosanagh Innes-Ker, Zara Phillips, Prince William of Wales, Laura Fellowes, Seamus Makim, Alice Ferguson, Peter Phillips, Lady Gabriella Windsor, Lord Frederick Windsor. *Second row:* Lady Sarah Armstrong-Jones, Princess Margaret, Princess Anne, Princess Diana holding Prince Henry, the Queen Mother, the Queen, the bride and groom, Major Ronald Ferguson, Prince Edward, Mrs. Hector Barrantes, the Hon. Mrs. Doreen Wright, Mrs. Jane Makim. *Slightly behind them:* Lady Elmhirst, Major Bryan Wright, Alexander Makim. *Third row:* Viscount Linley, Captain Mark Phillips, Marina Ogilvy, the Prince of Wales, Princess Alexandra, the Duke of Edinburgh, Princess Michael of Kent, Princess Alice, the Duchess of Gloucester, the Duchess of Kent, Lady Helen Windsor. *Back row:* James Ogilvy, Prince Michael of Kent, the Hon. Angus Ogilvy, the Duke of Gloucester, the Duke of Kent, and the Earl of St. Andrews.

# DEBRETT'S BOOK OF THE
# ROYAL
# WEDDING

### Jean Goodman

# DEBRETT'S PEERAGE LIMITED

LONDON. NEW YORK. SYDNEY. PERTH. W.A.
MCMLXXXVI

Copyright © Debrett's Peerage Limited 1986

ISBN 0 905649 91 5

Published by Debrett's Peerage Limited,
73–77 Britannia Road, London SW6 2JR.

*Represented by:*
Michael Joseph Limited
27 Wright's Lane
Kensington
London W8

*Distributed by:*
TBL Book Distribution Services
17–32 Nelson Way
Tuscan Trading Estate
Camberley
Surrey

Debrett's Book of the Royal Wedding

*Designed by:*
Vic Giolitto

*Picture Research:*
Anne-Marie Ehrlich

*Production
Management*
Facer Publishing
7 Colleton Crescent
Exeter EX2 4DG

*Typesetting:*
P&M Typesetting Ltd, Exeter

*Colour Reproduction:*
Peninsular Reproduction Services, Exeter

*Printed and bound by:*
Purnell Book Production Limited
Paulton, Bristol, England

# Contents

# Introduction

The Marriage which took place on Wednesday 23rd July 1986 at Westminster Abbey between Sarah Ferguson and His Royal Highness Prince Andrew The Duke of York was the culmination of a courtship and engagement which had captured the imagination of the British nation, and in the days leading up to the wedding, millions of others around the world.

In fact the worldwide television and radio audience which tuned into the wedding ceremony was estimated at between 300 and 500 million people, almost as many as had watched and heard the Heir to the throne marry Lady Diana Spencer five years earlier.

On the eve of the wedding day, the then Prince Andrew and Sarah Ferguson had given one of the most open and frank interviews ever recorded by members of the Royal Family, in which they each clearly expressed their strongly-held views and re-affirmed their love and respect for each other; not just in words, but in looks and gestures which were plain for all to see.

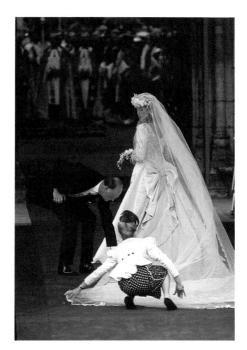

In fact that interview gave the most positive indication to date that the new Duchess of York is a very able and determined, but also a very sensitive person who seems ideally equipped to cope with the rigours of Royal life, and in the more immediate future, of being a Navy wife.

The confidence expressed by the plain 'Sarah Ferguson' on the eve of the wedding was echoed in her journey to Westminster Abbey the following day, and in the clear voice with which she made her vows. As she emerged from the Abbey as the new Duchess of York with her veil lifted from her smiling face, and her stunning titian hair shining in the sunlight under a diamond tiara, we were all suddenly aware that once again the Royal Family had gained yet another very valuable asset.

Here indeed was a worthy recruit to our fast expanding and increasingly popular Royal Family, and the subsequent scenes at Buckingham Palace, especially as the Duke and Duchess of York were leaving, clearly demonstrated her popularity within that family.

The wedding day had been full of the vitality and sense of fun for which the Duke and Duchess of York are renowned, and as they left for their honeymoon, anyone who had watched the proceedings, either in person, or

on television could not fail to think that here were two young people who really did seem to be 'made for each other'.

Their relationship had blossomed during a Windsor house party for Royal Ascot week in June 1985 to which the Princess of Wales had invited Sarah Ferguson. It developed, gently nurtured by the Prince and Princess of Wales, other members of the Royal Family and various mutual friends such as the Duke and Duchess of Roxburghe, until Prince Andrew finally proposed in the romantic surroundings of Floors Castle, in February this year, although the official announcement was not made until March 19th.

Prince Andrew's choice of bride found favour not only amongst members of the Royal Family, but amongst the nation as a whole. Even the hard-bitten national press warmed to this natural and fun-loving girl and quickly struck up a certain 'rapport' with her which has survived the four months of their engagement and was re-affirmed by the way they reported the preparations for, and the wedding itself. Long may this 'special relationship' continue and let us hope that the Duchess of York will never lose those qualities which have endeared her so much to us all.

For our part, Debrett's are once again proud to have documented such a happy Royal occasion as well as the lives and backgrounds of the Duke and Duchess of York, and the events leading up to their happy and glorious wedding day. It is a day which will be remembered for many years to come for its happiness and informality as well as for the spectacle. But it will be remembered most of all for the radiant beauty of the flame-haired girl who captured the heart of the nation as well as her Prince.

ROBERT JARMAN
MANAGING DIRECTOR
DEBRETT'S PEERAGE
JULY 1986

# The Engagement

'It is with great pleasure that the Queen and the Duke of Edinburgh announce the betrothal of their beloved son the Prince Andrew and Miss Sarah Ferguson, daughter of Major Ronald Ferguson and Mrs. Hector Barrantes.'

The ring. Prince Andrew and Sarah Ferguson show off her unique ruby and diamond engagement ring which they had chosen together. Sarah pronounced it 'stunning'.

This announcement, officially released from Buckingham Palace on the morning of Wednesday 19th March, 1986, ended the crescendo of speculation that had mounted during the previous six weeks. It had been expected that the news would be released at the traditional time of 11.00am,

but at 10.00am Miss Sarah Brennan, graduate of Exeter University, strode purposefully across the courtyard from the Palace press office and distributed a handful of typed notices to the reporters waiting at the gates. In the excitement a copy was seized by an onlooker's Old English sheepdog, Peggy, who made off with it, her owner in hot pursuit. It was noticed that the announcement had been dated 19th February (the date of Andrew's birthday) instead of 19th March.

Those two human incidents echoed the great sense of fun obviously shared by Prince Andrew and Sarah Ferguson. It showed in photographs taken when their engagement was announced and in their delighted happiness and relief which was apparent once their secret could be shared with the world.

During the weeks of unconfirmed rumours Sarah's three years' experience as a secretary with a public relations company had stood her in good stead when dealing with the press. Her unfailing good humour and the competent way she handled the reporters' persistent pursuit and fielded their questions won her their respect and admiration. In a strange way it was as if they recognised her as a former professional contact.

The pressure on her was enormous. On the night of Prince Andrew's twenty-sixth birthday, on 19th February, twenty photographers in nine cars chased her through London before she finally lost them in her BMW.

When Prince Andrew's ship docked at Portland an enterprising photographer sat down at the table next to her at lunchtime, at a little restaurant near her office, lifted his hands to show he had no camera and offered her a drink. She politely declined: 'Thank you; I must be getting back to work. I'm not being miserable or anything. Perhaps another time.'

Later that day as she left her office to post a letter she recognised the same photographer.

'If I'd known you were here I'd have got you to post the letter,' she told him conspiratorily. She had made a friend.

Prince Andrew proposed to Sarah, he said, while they were both guests of the Duke and Duchess of Roxburghe at Floors Castle, on the Scottish border, one of the most magnificent mansions in the country. The romantic turretted castle was featured by Warner Brothers in a Tarzan film. It is set in 60,000 acres on the banks of the River Tweed and was built by Sir John Vanbrugh in 1718 and partially rebuilt in Tudor times. It has often been a sanctuary for royalty and Prince Charles stayed there before his engagement to Princess Diana while, more recently, Prince Andrew entertained his former girl-friend there, the actress Koo Stark.

Sarah Ferguson travelled there to meet Prince Andrew in great secrecy, under the assumed name of Miss Anwell. It was the last weekend in February, a very wet weekend when, in a magnificent drawing-room filled with exquisite Belgian tapestries and fine French furniture, Prince Andrew dropped on to both his knees and asked Sarah to marry him.

To his surprise, he said, she said 'yes'. Sarah qualified her acceptance, however: 'If you wake up tomorrow morning, you can tell me it's all a huge joke,' she said. But Andrew was not joking. He immediately sought formal approval from the Queen, who had recently returned from her tour of Australia, and permission from Sarah's father, Major Ronald Ferguson, Prince Charles's fifty-four-year-old polo manager who had commanded the Sovereign's Escort of the Household Cavalry during his career in the Life Guards: Prince Andrew found that interview 'fairly nerveracking', although

Sarah Ferguson leaving for the last time the house in Clapham, South London, where she lived with her friend Caroline Beckwith-Smith. The formal announcement of the engagement was less than twenty-four hours away and from now on life would be dramatically different.

Danger! Men at Work. Sarah Ferguson is surrounded by photographers as she makes her way to the Mayfair art publishers where she worked. This is an example of the sort of pressure she was subjected to in the weeks leading up to the formal announcement of the engagement and which she coped with so well.

First inklings of a romance. The romance between Prince Andrew and Sarah Ferguson had taken everyone by surprise, and no one more so than the Prince himself. But Sarah Ferguson could hardly disguise her happiness in this photograph taken on the 8th January after she had spent Christmas with the Royal Family at Sandringham.

A Lady in Waiting. A radiant Sarah during the week before the engagement was announced.

he had known Major Ferguson, through polo, for a long time.

Major Ferguson was thrilled with his future son-in-law. 'He's a very fine person,' he said. 'I just hope he doesn't leave the Navy.... He's young, energetic, fully-trained, a damned good helicopter pilot by all account, and that's what he ought to do.'

Prince Andrew agreed. He had no intention, he said, of changing the course of his career and he planned to attend his three months' lieutenant's course at Greenwich Naval College. More surprisingly, Sarah intended to continue working with a London based graphics company for as long as was practicable. She enjoyed her work, she said, although it included 'making cups of coffee and doing most of the hoovering'.

The information came a few hours after the formal announcement of their engagement when Prince Andrew and Sarah Ferguson gave one of the happiest and most relaxed interviews to the press and television ever given by royalty. They held hands on the lawn of Buckingham Palace and when the camerman asked Sarah to give Prince Andrew a kiss she willingly agreed. 'Let's make it a smacker!' she said and kissed him on the lips.

'One is enough,' said the embarrassed Andrew, refusing a reporter's request for a second kiss.

But he and Sarah had proved that royal informality had travelled a long way since the day when the Prince of Wales stood on the Palace balcony on his wedding day and asked the Queen if it was all right to kiss his bride.

After their photo session in the grounds of Buckingham Palace, Prince Andrew and Sarah Ferguson sat side by side on a sofa in Andrew's

Sarah arriving for work the day before the engagement was announced. By this time press speculation had reached fever pitch.

sitting-room and showed off her unique ruby and diamond engagement ring – a large oval ruby surrounded by ten drop diamonds set in an eighteen-carat yellow and white gold band. It was valued by experts as worth at least £25,000.

Prince Andrew had helped to design it. 'We came to the mutual conclusion that red was probably the best colour for Sarah, and that is how we came to the choice of a ruby,' he said.

Sarah pronounced it 'stunning'.

It had been commissioned from the royal jewellers months ago when trays of rings were taken to the Palace along with designs on paper from which Prince Andrew suggested various refinements. The ring, which the jeweller described as being unlike any other in the world, was delivered to the Palace

Sarah's stepmother Susan Ferguson helped Sarah move out of her Clapham house.

Sarah on the way to work during the early days, before the press started taking the rumours of an imminent engagement seriously.

two days before the engagement announcement. It was not the first gift of jewellery Sarah had been given by Prince Andrew. Since Christmas she had consistently worn his present of a pair of heart-shaped diamond earrings.

Prince Andrew and Sarah Ferguson told reporters that although they had known each other for a long time their love story began at Royal Ascot, the previous June, when they sat near to each other at lunch. 'He made me eat chocolate profiteroles which I didn't want to eat at all,' she said. 'I was meant to be on a diet.'

Asked what they particularly liked about each other Sarah said 'wit,

Back at work the day after the announcement of the engagement but now surrounded by the sort of protection afforded to a member of the Royal Family. Prince Andrew's private bodyguard is on the right.

Stepping out to meet the press. Prince Andrew and Sarah Ferguson emerge from Buckingham Palace for the photographic session following the announcement of the engagement.

Stepping into the limelight; Prince Andrew and his fiancée Sarah Ferguson walk arm in arm through the grounds of Buckingham Palace, making their first public appearance as a betrothed couple.

Floors Castle from across the River Tweed. It was here that Prince Andrew proposed to Sarah Ferguson while they were staying as guests of the Duke and Duchess of Roxburghe.

The magnificent drawing-room of Floors Castle where Prince Andrew proposed to Sarah Ferguson.

A taste of things to come. A picture of the Royal Family at Buckingham Palace after the wedding of Prince Charles and Lady Diana Spencer (now the Princess of Wales). Prince Andrew was 'supporter' to Prince Charles.

charm and good looks'. Andrew added '...and red hair'. He said that during the past nine months they had discovered they were a good team who worked very well together. Sarah agreed, adding they were 'good friends...and very happy'.

Their engagement was greeted with great happiness across the world: the Queen was 'overjoyed', Prince Charles was 'delighted', Princes Anne said, 'I think my brother is an extremely lucky man', and in Australia the *Brisbane Courier Mail* claimed there was a 'Buckingham Palace sigh of relief for this perfect match'.

Among the first to hear the news were Prince Andrew's former shipmates on the frigate *Brazen*, berthed in Devonport for manoeuvres. The Prince telephoned the ship just before the time of the announcement and the occasion was celebrated there in champagne.

Champagne also flowed in the lovely Hampshire village of Dummer, at Sarah's family home, Dummer Down Farm, near the cottage of her grandmother, Lady Elmhurst, and in the village inn where the landlord, John Holland, distributed a special cocktail he had created for the occasion – 'Fergie's Fizz', a bubbly blend of champagne, orange juice, grenadine and Monterez liqueur. There they drank through the day and when darkness fell over the thatched roofs of the little cottages a special peal of bells rang from the twelfth-century parish church of All Saints – one of the prettiest churches in England according to the late Sir John Betjeman, the poet laureate. The peal sounded in joyous celebration that a friendly, cheery local girl was to marry a handsome prince.

# Andrew's Early Days

'People want their first child very much. They want their second almost as much. If a third child comes along they accept it as natural, but they haven't gone out of their way to try and get it.' So Prince Philip declared in a public speech some time after the birth of his third child.

It was a dull January day in 1960 when veteran midwife, Sister Helen Rowe, arrived in London to prepare for the arrival of a new royal baby. 'I have ordered two new overalls for my time at the Palace,' she said cheerfully, 'I always wear kingfisher blue – much nicer than nasty old grey.' Sister Rowe had already delivered Prince Charles and Princess Anne, but this new child was to be rather different. It would be the first born to a reigning British monarch for over a hundred years – since Queen Victoria's youngest daughter, Princess Beatrice, was born in 1857.

Prince Andrew with royal nannies.

Prince Andrew struggling to mount a toy dog.

On 19th February at 4.15pm the crowds clustered expectantly around the railings at Buckingham Palace and a great cheer went up when a servant came from the Palace and pinned up a notice which announced, 'The Queen was safely delivered of a son at 3.30pm today. Her Majesty and the infant Prince are both doing well.' The new baby's arrival immediately created a reshuffle in the order of succession to the Throne. He was ranked immediately after his brother, the eleven-year-old Prince Charles, and so displaced his sister, Princess Anne, then aged ten. The new prince was to occupy this position for twenty-two years.

He weighed in at seven pounds three ounces – three ounces lighter than Prince Charles was at birth – and a team of four physicians, headed by Lord Evans, was in attendance as well as Sister Rowe. But as with the birth of Prince Charles, no government representative was there to check on the newborn baby in accordance with the old custom dating from the day of James II whose second wife, Mary of Modena, was rumoured to have smuggled a changeling into the bedroom, in a warming pan.

The Queen was thirty-three and the birth took place in the Belgian Suite

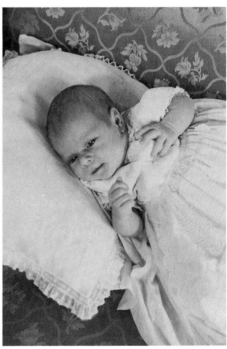

The first official photograph of Prince Andrew taken by Cecil Beaton in the blue drawing-room at Buckingham Palace. Prince Andrew was born on 19th February, 1960.

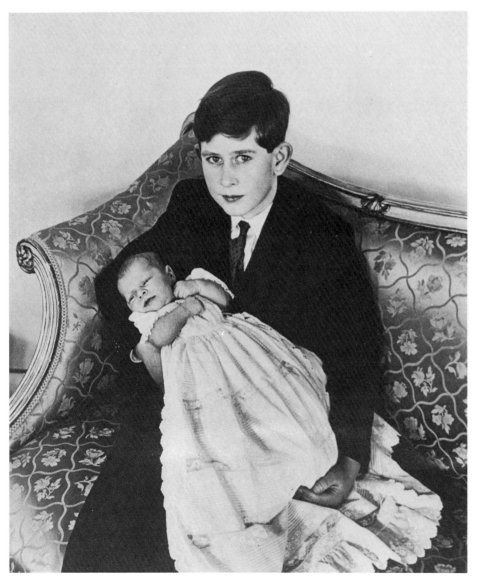

The proud elder brother. Prince Charles holds his young brother for Cecil Beaton's camera and already displays a professional approach towards formal sittings of this kind.

on the ground floor of Buckingham Palace, overlooking the gardens. The Duke of Edinburgh was upstairs in his study. The first to be told, he rushed downstairs shouting 'it's a boy' to everyone within hearing distance and later took Princess Anne to see her mother and new brother. He also telephoned Princes Charles at Cheam School who, that night, was driven to the Palace to see the newest member of his family. His grandmother, the Queen Mother, arrived from Clarence House with Princess Margaret, soon to be married to Antony Armstrong-Jones. Other early visitors included Princess Marina, the widowed Duchess of Kent, with her daughter Princess Alexandra.

Army salutes to the new prince were fired in Hyde Park, the Tower of London, Windsor Castle, Cardiff Castle and from the battleship *Vanguard*, dressed over all, while the Black Arrows of the Royal Air Force staged a fly-past of thirty-six Hunter jets. Sirens tooted from tugs on the Thames and the bells rang from St Paul's Cathedral and from churches throughout the country.

The details of the baby's weight, his blue eyes and light brown hair were public knowledge but his names remained a secret for more than a month, until 22nd March when his birth was registered. This perhaps indicated the Queen's determination that her second son should receive as little press or public attention as possible. She felt that she and Princess Margaret had both enjoyed a relatively secluded childhood but Prince Charles and Princess Anne had often been alarmed and inhibited by the glare of the cameras. Prince

Prince Andrew applauds his baby brother Prince Edward; this photograph was taken in one of the sitting-rooms at Windsor Castle.

Prince Andrew, in cowboy jacket, holds on to the royal corgis, while the Queen admires them.

Alone with a lollipop in a side window of Buckingham Palace, four-year-old Prince Andrew watches the Trooping the Colour.

Prince Andrew seated beside his elder sister, displaying an early confidence.

The Royal Family in the grounds of Frogmore, Windsor. Prince Andrew seemed to be developing an early interest in horticulture.

Helping with the leaves. Prince Andrew with young brother Edward and corgis in the grounds of Buckingham Palace.

The Queen and Prince Andrew return from Sandringham after the Christmas holidays.

All dressed up and somewhere to go. Prince Andrew, aged seven, at King's Cross station waiting to leave for Balmoral where the whole Royal Family traditionally spend their summer holidays.

Birthday Boy. This photograph of Prince Andrew was taken in the grounds of Buckingham Palace just before his 6th birthday on February, 19th, 1966.

Andrew Albert Christian Edward should have a comparatively private childhood.

He was a month old before the first formal photographs were issued to the newspapers. They were taken by Cecil Beaton. In those days Palace formality could be overpowering. The Queen and Prince Philip with their three children grouped themselves in the Nash rooms. Beaton was anxious to get some inspired photographs and afterwards wrote in his diary.

'I felt as if I were being chased in a nightmare when one's legs sink into the mire. The family stood to attention. I said something to make them smile, so clicked. I clicked like mad at anything that seemed even passable. The baby, thank God, behaved itself and did not cry or spew. It sometimes opened its eyes. But even so I felt the odds tremendously against me. The weight of the Palace crushed me. The opposition of "this hearty Naval type" must be contended with, and due deference to the Queen....'

The odds lessened when everyone but Sister Rowe with Prince Andrew departed because, according to Beaton's biographer, Hugo Vickers, it seemed Prince Philip had annoyed the photographer by making suggestions including 'Take it from here. Why not there?' Beaton told him why quite firmly. Eventually the Prince wanted to borrow Beaton's lights and take pictures himself.

Prince Charles, Beaton thought, seemed very overawed by the atmosphere

Reviewing the flypast from the balcony on Buckingham Palace following the Trooping the Colour ceremony in 1966, aged six, from left to right: Lord Mountbatten in great military splendour, Princess Margaret, the Queen Mother and Lord Linley, the son of Princess Margaret and Lord Snowdon; Andrew in the centre wears collar and tie and has an expression of open-mouthed, narrow-eyed keen observation which remained with him throughout his growing up.

The first official engagement. Prince Andrew, aged eight, impressed everyone with the way he carried out his duties. A member of the 1st St Marylebone pack, he wore his cub scout uniform for the march past of a thousand Queen's Scouts, and before the parade he needed only a slight adjustment of his red and black neckerchief for his turnout to win the approval of the Duke of Edinburgh and the Chief Scout, Sir Charles Maclean.

'as if awaiting a clout from behind, or for his father to tweak his ear or pull the tuft of hair at the crown of his head'.

Finally, Prince Philip broke up the session by saying, 'Surely we've had enough. If he's not got what he wants by now he's an even worse photographer than I think he is. Ha! Ha!' Beaton wrote:

'I then threw myself upon the mercies of Sister Rowe. She was splendid and would have done anything to help me get good results. She would have even given the baby a vodka cocktail to keep it awake. As it was she pinched it, jerked its hand, thumped its back and it was while she nursed it by the window that we got what I felt were the best results.'

Beaton photographed Prince Andrew lying on some Philip de Salle silk surrounded by speckled carnations, lilies of the valley and spring flowers. The Queen released nine photographs for publication but not the ones which Beaton considered the best. However, those nine were the last pictures of the baby prince the public would see for a long time.

No christening ones were released after the ceremony conducted on 8th April by the Archbishop of Canterbury. The silver-gilt font designed by Prince Albert was brought from the Gold Pantry at Windsor to the gold and white Music Room at Buckingham Palace which had been temporarily transformed into a chapel for the occasion. For his baptism Prince Andrew wore the traditional christening robe of Honiton lace over a satin petticoat which Queen Victoria had had made in 1842 for the christening of her second child, the future King Edward VII.

The Royal Family on the balcony of Buckingham Palace following the Trooping the Colour ceremony. Prince Andrew leans over the balcony observing the crowds below.

A keen observer. Prince Andrew watching the polo at Windsor with a glamorous companion.

A few days before Prince Andrew's birth, the Queen had changed her children's surname from Windsor to Mountbatten-Windsor, by Royal decree, in fairness to Prince Philip. The new prince was named Andrew (after Prince Philip's father), Albert (after the Queen's father before he came to the throne as George VI), Christian (after Prince Philip's great-grandfather, King Christian IX of Denmark) and Edward (after King Edward VII, the Queen's great-grandfather).

His godparents were the Duke of Gloucester, (the Queen's last surviving paternal uncle, who died in 1974), the Queen's first cousin, Princess Alexandra of Kent, Lord Elphinstone, (her first cousin on her mother's side, who died in 1975), the Earl of Euston (later 11th Duke of Grafton) whose wife was a Lady of the Bedchamber to the Queen and later Mistress of the Robes; and Mrs Harold Phillips, another close personal friend of the Royal Family.

For the first sixteen months of his life the first prince to be called Andrew since the 1707 Act of Union with Scotland was never seen in public. Gradually, even the joyous Scots, who were delighted that the little prince shared the name of their patron saint, were concerned that there was 'something wrong' with the baby they never saw.

At nearly six months old he was included in an official photograph taken for the Queen Mother's sixtieth birthday. By then he showed every sign of being the most extrovert and outgoing of the three royal children. His nanny, Mabel Anderson, who had been in charge of the royal nurseries since Princess Anne was born, found him remarkably placid and content and full of fun.

His mother organised her day so that she spent more time with him than she had with either of her elder children. She was with him every morning for half an hour after breakfast, nursed and played with him again for half an hour at mid-morning and dashed upstairs to his nursery or wheeled him in his pram in the garden whenever she was free during the afternoon.

Evening engagements were cut to a minimum so that she could bath and feed him and settle him down for the night. Often Prince Philip joined them at that time.

Sister Rowe gave regular progress reports to assure the public that Andrew was 'full of smiles' and 'simply wonderful in every respect'. The rumours spread, however, until he made his first public appearance on the balcony of Buckingham Palace on the second Saturday of June 1961 after Trooping the Colour. Held in his mother's arms, clearly seen against the scarlet tunic she had worn for the ceremony, he pointed at the massed crowds and craned backwards to watch a squadron of Javelin fighters roaring a salute from the skies. The public were satisfied.

Informality, however, was the keynote of those early days and he responded and grew into an exubrant and mischievous toddler.

He spent far more time with his mother than either his brother or sister had. A supply of toys was kept in the bottom drawer of an antique bureau in her study and often, while she worked at her desk on official papers, he could be found playing happily on the floor.

When he was two years old his mother gave him his first lessons. Every morning after breakfast she taught him to count, recite his ABC and tell the time by means of a small blackboard incorporating a clock face and a counting frame which was kept in the private drawing-room. She gave him

Prince Andrew watching his father playing polo at Windsor Great Park in April 1968, aged eight. It was at one of these polo meetings that he would have met Sarah Ferguson for the very first time while her father, then Captain Ronald Ferguson, was playing polo with Prince Philip.

his first riding lessons, holding him on the back of a small Shetland pony which she walked round the yard in the Royal Mews. Meanwhile Prince Philip taught him to swim in the palace's covered pool, sail at Cowes, and he joined Princess Anne's weekly dancing class.

His world extended to include family holidays at Windsor, Sandringham and Balmoral and, by the time he was 'three and a big bit', as he described himself, other boys came regularly to the palace to play.

Guests at his fourth birthday party included his cousin, Viscount Linley (Princess Margaret's son), the Earl of St Andrews (The Duke of Kent's son), Philip Astor (grandson of the 1st Lord Astor of Hever), Henry Tennant (grandson of 2nd Lord Glenconner) and Coco the Clown who provided the entertainment. Soon afterwards his brother Edward Antony Richard Louis was born. Andrew's immediate family was complete.

Meanwhile his education started in earnest with lessons in the improvised schoolroom in the palace under the royal governess Katherine Peebles, a Scot who had taught Charles his first lessons. Andrew was joined by two boys, Justin Beaumont and James Steel, and two girls, Katie Seymour, whose father was the director of a brewing concern and an extra equerry to the Queen Mother, and Victoria Butler, the daughter of Lord Dunbayne. Later Andrew's younger cousin David, Lord Linley, joined the class.

Apart from the 'three R's' Miss Peebles taught her pupils history, scripture and geography and, later, French. Prince Andrew also had piano and skating

A group of royal children at Windsor Castle. (from left to right): James Ogilvy, Lady Sarah Armstrong-Jones, Earl of St Andrews, Lady Helen Windsor, Viscount Linley, Prince Andrew, Marina Ogilvy, Prince Edward, with Prince Charles and Princess Anne at the back.

Sarah Ferguson gives Prince Andrew (with back to camera) an admiring glance in this early photograph of them taken at Windsor Great Park.

lessons and, as he grew older, he was secretly taken to Lords and Wimbledon for private coaching in cricket from Ken Muncer, and tennis from the former champion Dan Maskell.

There were secret holidays too with his schoolroom companion Katie Seymour at her parents' holiday home on the Isle of Wight where no photographer thought of looking for him.

Life for the young prince was full and exciting. Probably because he was protected from the public attention endured by Charles and Anne, he developed into a natural extrovert which, allied to a love of practical jokes inherited from his father, often caused trouble in the household.

He demonstrated his newly-acquired skill at tying his own shoe laces to

The young Prince Andrew having an intimate conversation with a royal corgi.

the palace guards on sentry duty by tying their bootlaces together; he switched round the direction signs at a palace garden party; poured bubble bath into the Windsor swimming pool and drove his pedal car into a pack of the Queen's corgis. During the ceremony of changing the guard at Balmoral the guard commander saluted smartly and requested the Queen's permission to march off. 'I do wish Mummy would say "No" for a change,' Andrew was heard to comment loudly.

In bad weather he kicked his football about in Buckingham Palace's long upstairs corridor. 'Every now and again a pane of glass got broken,' he later admitted, 'but I don't think we ever broke a piece of Meissen or anything like that.'

Mabel Anderson found him a handful after the docile and affectionate Charles and Anne. It seemed the astrologers might be proved right when they predicted that, as an Aquarian on the cusp of Pisces, born when Mars was in conjunction with Venus, he would grow up to be lively, warm, full of fun and attractive to women. Certainly Mabel Anderson was so devoted to him that she could rarely be persuaded to take her days off.

*The young Prince Andrew having an intimate conversation with a royal corgi.*

# A Prince in the Making

Despite Prince Andrew's outgoing and adventurous personality his parents were determined to keep him out of the public eye for as long as possible. He was smuggled to a private gymnasium for physical education and taken secretly to the Brigade of Guards' sports ground for football and athletics with a select group of his contemporaries.

The 1st Marylebone Wolf Cub Pack was by no means as select and it gave Prince Andrew his first chance to mix with boys from very different backgrounds. Unfortunately, his parents were so worried in case his presence at their meetings attracted publicity that they were transferred to the palace, where every week for six months the whole pack arrived in a mini-bus. He so

Boarding school for Prince Andrew. At the age of eight he was sent to Heatherdown, a private boarding school at Ascot, only about seven miles away from Windsor Castle.

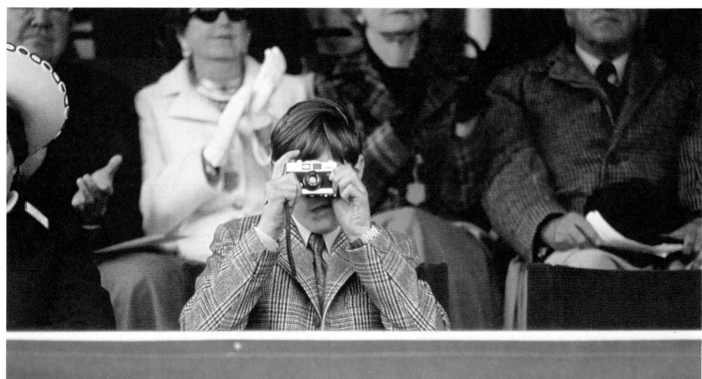

At the Duke of Beaufort's estate, at Badminton, Gloucestershire. Prince Andrew is in the company, from left to right, of Lady Helen Windsor, daughter of the Duke and Duchess of Kent, and Lady Sarah Armstrong-Jones and Viscount Linley, the children of Princess Margaret and Lord Snowdon.

Prince Andrew seated between the Queen and the Queen Mother at the Royal Braemar Highland Gathering, near Balmoral (usually referred to as the Braemar Games).

The young photographer. Prince Andrew displays an early interest in photography, which was to become more serious as he grew older.

enjoyed the Wolf Cub meetings that it was obvious it was time for him to mix with more boys of his own age. The question of schooling could no longer be delayed.

Boarding school offered more privacy from the press than a day school, and at eight and a half Andrew went as a boarder to Heatherdown, a private preparatory school for some ninety boys up to the age of thirteen. The young prince seemed eager to substitute it for the quiet seclusion of the Buckingham Palace schoolroom.

He had been expected to follow Prince Charles to Cheam School, Headley, on the Berkshire Downs but Charles had been unhappy there, partly perhaps because of the constant presence of the press, and the Queen's Press Secretary stressed that Andrew should not have to go through the same ordeal. Heatherdown was not entirely an unknown quantity; because the Hon. Angus Ogilvy, husband of Princess Alexandra, had been there, and had already put his five-year-old son, James, down for the school where he himself had been very happy.

The headmaster, Mr James Edwards, confirmed the Queen's and Prince Philip's wishes that the young prince should have a normal school life.

'It is a great honour for the school,' he said,. 'but he will receive the same treatment here as all the other boys.'

He explained he was not opposed to corporal punishment but seldom administered it and he detested giving lines because they were 'so bad for the handwriting'.

Rugger Royal. Prince Andrew enjoying rugger practice with school friends at Heatherdown. As soon as lessons were over the boys would don pairs of green overalls over their uniform and take to the playing fields.

Prince Andrew in the thick of it. Andrew, the tallest player in the scrum (centre), does his utmost to get to the ball in a match between Heatherdown, his prep school, and another school near Windsor.

Wolf cubs at the Palace. Eight-year-old Prince Andrew (left) and one of the pack doing the 'Grand Howl' which starts the meeting. This was his last meeting with the 1st St Marylebone Cub Scout Pack before he started school at Heatherdown in September 1968.

Pensive Prince. Andrew concentrates intensely at some horse trials. Despite this apparent love of horses, he has never displayed his elder brother's aptitude for polo.

'Each child,' he said, 'is treated in a different way. Some might be beaten if the occasion arose, whereas with others it might do more harm than good. Some do prep in the evenings, others don't. They begin playing games like rugby when they are physically ready, not just when they reach a certain age.'

The gaunt Victorian building seven miles from Windsor is set in thirty acres of grounds and has excellent sports facilities including a swimming pool and a miniature shooting range. Fees were £157 a term.

Andrew, equipped with the uniform grey jacket and trousers, red and black blazer, cap and tie, shared a dormitory for six, got up at 7.15 every day and received a sound grounding in English, Maths, History, Geography, Science, Biology, Scripture, French, Latin, Music and Carpentry, from 9.00am to 12.30pm. In the afternoon there were games until supper at 6.00pm followed by bed at 8.00pm. Boys were occasionally allowed to watch television and were free to go home for one weekend a term. If they were not involved in sport they were allowed to go out with their parents on Saturday afternoons. For Andrew and his friends this often meant a trip home with his parents for tea at Windsor Castle. The only concession made to his Royal status was the security man who was never far behind.

Security became more obvious early in 1971 when the police learned of an IRA plot to kidnap George, Earl of St Andrews, son of the Duke and Duchess of Kent, who had followed his cousin, Andrew, to Heatherdown. A strict twenty-four hour guard was mounted on the school buildings and although the boys regarded it as a great joke, the threat was serious.

After security was relaxed Andrew's bodyguard proved his usefulness when a party of Heatherdown boys visited the Natural History Museum in London and became involved in a fight with other youngsters. The scuffle had nothing to do with Andrew but his security man helped the museum attendants to break it up.

Andrew soon became the leader of his own group of friends and often led them into mischief.

Taking the salute. Prince Andrew in the cub scout uniform of the 1st St Marylebone pack.

Prince Andrew relaxing on the moors at Balmoral.

Strolling between the cars during a polo match at Windsor. Prince Andrew follows the young Sarah Ferguson and friend, hotly pursued by Sarah Armstrong-Jones.

Prince Andrew sailing off the Nova Scotia coast, Canada.

Quiet observation. Prince Andrew in the back of a Range Rover watching the world go by.

'He was sometimes aggressive, often obstinate, always confident and competitive,' according to his biographers Graham and Heather Fisher.

'Charles in schooldays,' they wrote, had been easy to handle, readily doing what he was told, nervous of putting a foot wrong. Andrew, by contrast, was 'sometimes a bit of a handful! There was a bit of "I am the Prince" about him when he first arrived,' one of the boys recalled, '. . . it was soon knocked out of him. The ribbings he got were unmerciful and he caught on fast. He had to.'

A schoolfriend particularly remembers his generosity: on birthdays it was usual for boys to give their close friends a slice of birthday cake. Andrew, who received a particularly large cake, gave a piece to every boy in the school. This unprecedented gesture, from all reports, has never been repeated.

He was perhaps best remembered at Heatherdown for shinning up the school flagpole and tying a shirt to the top of the mast, and for the formation of a School Scout Cub Pack, as a result of his enthusiastic activity with the Marylebone Pack. He loved enterprising outdoor activities and, at thirteen, was an ideal candidate for his father's old school Gordonstoun, on the north-east coast of Scotland, although Charles had not been happy there.

The remote Morayshire boarding school, which more conventional public schoolboys dismissed as 'a gymnasium of morals and muscles', reflected the belief of its founder Kurt Hahn, a German Jew, jailed by the Nazis for criticising their murderous policies. He was released only on the personal intervention of Ramsay MacDonald. Its motto 'There is More in You' reflected Hahn's conviction that character came from learning to endure hardship, exhaustion and cold without grumbling or, worst still in the case of new boys, bursting into tears. Only through testing and stretching oneself, he believed, could self awareness to become mature, responsible adults be achieved.

Greetings to Canada. Prince Andrew is met on his arrival at Toronto airport by Lieutenant-Governor Pauline McGibbon and her husband Donald McGibbon. The sixteen-year-old Prince attended the private boys' school, Lakefield College, near Peterborough, Ontario, where he was staying for a six-months' exchange trip.

Happy holiday. Prince Andrew spent a week at Bembridge, Isle of Wight, with Major and Mrs Raymond Seymour, friends of the Royal family. Most of the time was spent on the sands with the Seymour's nine-year-old daughter Katy with whom Andrew became friends when she attended private lessons with him at Buckingham Palace.

Gordonstoun School, Elgin near Perth, where Prince Andrew went after Heatherdown, and where he thrived on the spartan regime and all the outdoor activities.

Kurt Hahn, the legendary founder of Gordonstoun who left a great impression on all the boys under his care.

Since Prince Philip's day, when all the boys wore short trousers and followed a spartan regime of cold showers, long runs and strenuous physical exercise, the emphasis on physical endurance had, under a new headmaster, John Kempe, leader of the 1954 Kungchenjunga Expedition, been considerably toned down. A disco evening was allowed five or six times a term, swots were tolerated, so were girl pupils, but everyone had to do some form of community service and support the school theatre. In line with its aims in outdoor community service, Gordonstoun also had a twenty-five fire brigade team which was part of the Grampian Region fire service, and a mountain rescue team which was responsible for an area in the Cairngorms.

Prince Andrew found the early-morning run reduced to a mere dash in shorts only, around the goalposts during the summer. The school however, kept its reputation for outdoor activities, particularly sailing. It is three miles from Hopeman Harbour and in Prince Andrew's day it was compulsory for every new boy or girl to spend a week with Commander Edelston and Chief Petty Officer 'Barney' Robinson, to get a taste of the sea. Andrew already had his own light aluminium craft at Balmoral and had loved the sea from an early age. Senior pupils also manned a coastguard watch-tower, had the use of the school yacht, *Sea Spirit*, and formed their own in-shore rescue team.

Andrew and his 6'2" blond detective, Mr Topless, were taken to Gordonstoun by the Queen and Prince Philip. However, the thirteen-year-old tall, good-looking, new boy's reputation was enhanced when, almost immediately, he was seen in animated conversation with an attractive

Prince Andrew relaxing with the Trudeau family during his six-month exchange trip to Canada.

Prince Andrew talking to children in Nova Scotia. The young Canadian boy on the ground is obviously an aspiring photographer.

The Royal family in Canada during 1976. This was the year that Prince Andrew went to Lakefield College, Ontario, on a six months exchange visit from Gordonstoun.

sixteen-year-old blonde Amanda Knatchbull. It was some time before the other boys realised that the granddaughter of Earl Mountbatten of Burmah was Andrew's cousin.

In his first terms he was often a conspicuous running round the lawn in front of the school on Wednesday and Saturday afternoons – a penalty drill carried out in silence for a period of from five minutes to an hour according to the offence. Andrew's penalty was invariably for larking around in the dormitory.

'He was forever getting penalized,' recalled Richard Boyle whose younger brother Rupert was in Cumming House, with Andrew.

Rupert and Andrew had arrived as new boys together. One night soon afterwards, they were playing 'dormitory rugby' when Rupert tackled Andrew who tripped, hit a partition wall with his head and, the next morning, went along to the school matron with a bad headache. He had a lump on his head and was sent to hospital to be X-rayed. There was no serious damage but afterwards the house master, Peter Larkman, called Rupert into his study.

'You really shouldn't have done that,' he said. 'If the X-ray result had been serious you and I would have been sent to the Tower for treason.'

Andrew's royal status was hardly apparent apart from the unobtrusive presence of Detective Topless who slept in the sanatorium and, unless accompanying the prince on out-of-school events, spent most of his time participating in school life by helping with outdoor activities.

The Cowboy Prince. During his visit to Canada Prince Andrew, aged seventeen, entered into the spirit of things by dressing in cowboy gear for this particular event.

At home on the range. Prince Andrew spent the Easter holidays away from Lakefield College on the farm of a schoolfriend, Peter Lorriman. The farm, about eighty miles from Toronto, provided plenty of opportunity for Andrew to experience the Canadian way of life.

Canadian adventure. Prince Andrew proved that Britain still ruled the waves when he stripped to the waist to go canoeing in Canada. In fact he spent a very arduous few weeks canoeing through the Canadian lakes with a group of friends from Lakefield College.

The first of many. Prince Andrew with Sarah Johnson, the first pretty young lady in whose company Andrew was photographed. He is obviously making some emphatic statement at the Commonwealth Games which were held at Stormont, Canada, in July 1976.

'It was strange, however, Richard Boyle said, 'to see a photograph of the Queen and Prince Philip signed "Mum and Dad" beside a bed in the dormitory.'

Andrew's most exciting Gordonstoun experiences started at fifteen with an Air Training Corps gliding course at Lossiemouth. He made his first glider flight there, a four-minute circuit of Milltown airfield, with Flight Lieutenant Sandy Reid in a two-seater training glider. His instructor noted that he was fearless and quick to learn. The next year he flew solo for the first time and qualified for his ATC glider proficiency wings. He probably prized them more than his six 'O' levels. They were for English Language and Literature, Mathematics, General Science, British History and French, a

Prince Andrew chatting with the father of a schoolfriend, Peter Lorriman, on whose farm he stayed near Toronto.

Scoring a hit with a group of Canadian girls. Prince Andrew has always had a way with the ladies.

Prince Charles and Prince Andrew entering into the spirit of things at the Calgary Stampede.

Prince Andrew preparing to fly an American helicopter in San Diego, California.

Prince Andrew inspecting a Guard of Honour in Canada.

A peaked cap shades his eyes against the glare as Prince Andrew arrives at Coppermine River at the start of his canoe trip into the lonely North-West Territory.

language which no doubt had benefited from his three weeks' exchange visit with a party of fiteen Gordonstoun boys to a Jesuit College near Toulouse.

Security precautions were strict and there was no mention of the visit in either the English or French press until he was back in England. Only then was it learned that he had been recognised by a French reporter but had told him, in near honesty, 'My name is Andrew Edwards. My father is a gentleman farmer and my mother does not work.'

There were several 'secret' journeys abroad: he learned to ski in Germany completely unrecognised and without the media harassment that had tormented Charles. His father piloted him to Germany several times to visit his relations, and no journalists were waiting to greet him at Oban when he was one of the crew who sailed the school ketch *Sea Spirit* round Scotland in rough weather.

Later that term he made his acting debut in a school production of the farce *Simple Spyman*. He had a minor role and, unlike Charles's attempts at amateur dramatics, it was hardly noticed. His parents had achieved the seemingly impossible task of letting him live a near normal life, well out of the limelight. When he emerged into the glare of public life for the first time at the age of sixteen, his friendly infectious grin, his enthusiasm and his mature confidence proved they had been right. He was ready to face whatever life might offer.

It was at the 1976 Montreal Olympics that he made his first real impact. He flew out to join his parents on the royal yacht *Britannia*, the longest journey

he had made to date, and arrived in Canada to be hailed as something of a glamour boy. *Woman's Own* gushed: 'If they'd handed out Gold Medals for sex appeal . . . Britain would have cakewalked it . . . and the recipient would have been Prince Andrew.'

Thousands of teenagers went to the Olympic Games just to catch a glimpse of him and astonished members of the Royal party had letters, invitations, love poems and photographs of the senders addressed to him, pressed into their hands. Wherever the Royal family went he captured all the attention.

Andrew was the undoubted star. He was pretending not to notice but he was certainly well aware of what was going on!' commented a British journalist.

His official escort was sixteen-year-old Sandi Jones, the self-possessed daughter of Colonel Campbell Jones, director-general of the Olympic yachting events. Her envious friends described her as 'the luckiest girl alive'. When asked her opinion of her guest, she simply said, 'the Prince is very nice.'

The Canadian visit prompted the idea of a two-term exchange visit at Lakefield College, seventy miles from Toronto. The school of 250 boys had been influenced by the Gordonstoun system and had run an exchange scheme with it for some years. So after another term at Gordonstoun

Prince Andrew, gregarious as always, flashes his famous smile and sports the T-shirt of his Canadian school, Lakefield College, as he embarks at Southampton for a holiday at Balmoral.

The young princes. Three well dressed young men attend the Farnborough Air Show in 1978.

Prince Andrew with two Canadian beauties at the Calgary Stampede.

Andrew was back in Canada at the start of 1977 for an experience that was a counterpart of Charles' period in Australia at Timbertops and Geelong School, twelve years previously.

Andrew was in his element: he revelled in his first ever press conference. 'This is the first time I've done this sort of thing,' he admitted gleefully. I'm only a nipper – not considered old enough for press interviews.'

He admitted he was something of a comedian – 'It seems to run in the family'. As for girls? He 'liked them as much as the next guy'.

He was in Wadsworth House, a red-painted timber-framed building, supervised by a former ice-hockey star, then the school's head of economics and director of athletics. His room mate was an old friend, Donald Grant who had been an exchange scholar at Gordonstoun two years previously. They had met while Grant was unpacking in the dormitory.

'I didn't recognize him,' Grant said. 'We had been talking for about fifteen minutes when I looked down and saw HRH and his name on his trunk. We became friends. He was very natural – just one of the boys there. I carried on calling him Andrew.'

So did his new Canadian friends who sometimes contracted it to Andy and later, because of his amazing popularity with the girls, to 'Randy Andy'.

He scored two goals in his first game of ice hockey and collected a mass of bruises. His performance even surprised David Miller, Lakefield's head boy.

'He was pretty good,' he said. "He was quite vicious too, and you need to be a bit vicious to be good at this game.'

He ski-ied himself into the school's second team and played fullback for the first rugby XV, cheered on by girls in T-shirts proclaiming across their chests I'M AN ANDY WINDSOR GIRL. But the only Canadian girl he dated repeatedly was Sandi Jones, the pretty teenager who had guided him round the 1976 Olympics.

He invited her to his school dance and stayed by her side all evening. Two months later they dined in Toronto and went to a jazz concert. He took her ski-ing and persuaded his detective to let them go alone on condition he kept in touch by a walkie-talkie.

'There wasn't much romancing under the eye of Andrew's bodyguards,' Sandi complained, 'though we managed to give them the slip on occasions. Andrew can be extremely resourceful. He's just an ordinary guy who wants to have a fun time with his girlfriend . . . we get on together fabulously.'

He did have fun; running, wind-surfing, curling, canoeing and hurtling down the bob sleigh run from the school to the frozen lake. He also acted with the school's dramatic society with no conspicuous success. During the Easter vacation he stayed with a school friend, Peter Lorrimer, on his father's farm and tried his hand at maple-tapping.

Despite the wealth of distractions he kept his work up to standard and

The famous paint-spraying incident when Prince Andrew jokingly turned on American journalists and photographers while inspecting a housing rehabilitation project in the black ghetto district of Watts, Los Angeles.

Prince Andrew and Prince Charles arriving at St Paul's for the wedding day on 29th July, 1981.

passed comfortably the various examinations comparable to those in the lower VI form in an English school.

He flew home for his mother's Silver Jubilee celebrations but returned to Canada for an intensive cross-country tour followed by a strenuous Arctic adventure with Lakefield's headmaster, Terry guest, and a small group of boys. It was a 200-mile trip down the Coppermine River to the Arctic Ocean in two-man canoes; a demanding journey even for experienced canoeists through treacherous currents and over hazardous rapids and falls. The food and camping equipment were carried in the canoes and every evening, for two and a half weeks, they pitched camp in all weather conditions and fished the river to supplement their dehydrated food.

Andrew revelled in the tough challenge that took him through desolate country where man seems an intruder. Every day brought its share of mishaps and when a canoe capsized its crew found themselves in near-freezing water. Day by day he paddled on, ignoring plagues of flies and agonising blisters. The most dangerous moment was shooting the rapids near Rocky Defile which not all Coppermine explorers survive.

He returned to Gordonstoun for his final year, physically tougher and with his character and outlook widened and strengthened by Canada, ready

The Queen and her second son. Prince Andrew leans forward to speak to his mother while the Queen keeps her attention fixed on the course during the Badminton Horse Trials.

The Polo Princes. Charles and Andrew deep in conversation during a polo match at Windsor Great Park.

Prince Andrew at twenty-one. Andrew photographed in the grounds of Buckingham Palace on the eve of his twenty-first birthday in 1981.

to take his three 'A' levels and cope with an endless series of would-be girlfriends.

He sat his 'A' levels under a *nom de plume*, at his father's suggestion, and passed in history, English, Economics and Political Studies. The succession of girls known as 'Andrew's Harem' ensured the continuation of his nick-name Randy Andy.

One minute he's making your feel really great . . . that you're the only one that matters,' one said. 'The next minute, just as you really think you're getting somewhere, he's off with somebody else.'

His real love affair at that time was with Canada and the next year he was back for the Commonwealth Games.

His memories of the country were recorded in a series of abstract landscape paintings. When they were exhibited in a Windsor festival the art critic of the *Sunday Telegraph* said he showed 'an adventurous sense of abstraction and composition beyond the usual admirable amateurism of royal performances.' Allied to his love of pottery, which he had pursued at Gordonstoun and Lakefield, they showed an unexpected artistic side to his character.

At Gordonstoun he had been head of his house, captained the cricket XI and played for it for three years, been in the First XI hockey team and gained a gold in the Duke of Edinburgh's award scheme. Unlike his father and Charles, however, he had not been head of school: for the first time in Gordonstoun's history that honour went to a girl.

In the school holidays he had taken a crash course in flying at RAF Benson and flown solo in a naval Chipmunk. He had also parachuted from a Hercules aircraft after a two-weeks' training course.

'Of course I was nervous,' he admitted. 'If you're not nervous you do something stupid. But I'm dead keen to do it again.'

He was excellently prepared to begin training as a naval helicopter pilot and enlist in the Navy for a twelve-year term. In September 1979 he reported to Britannia Royal Naval College, Dartmouth for a seven-months' indoctrination period in naval traditions and attitudes. His first order was 'Get your hair cut!'

Lady Diana (just before her marraige to Prince Charles in 1981) accompanying Prince Andrew in the procession for the Trooping the Colour.

Prince Andrew preparing to inspect a Guard of Honour in Canada.

# A Naval Career –
# The Falklands

Prince Andrew on board HMS *Brazen*.

Prince Andrew arrived at Dartmouth with one of the two security officers, Inspector Steve Burgess, who would accompany him nearly everywhere during his training, even on a thirty-mile route march over a marine assault course when Andrew waded, waist high with full equipment, through icy water and slept rough in the middle of Dartmoor. He thought he was fit but he lost more than seven pounds in weight in his first month's basic training.

After two months' naval initiation at Dartmouth he flew to the United States with nineteen other midshipmen to join the aircraft carrier *Hermes* at naval air bases at Pensacola, Fort Lauderdale and Bermuda. It seemed he was not as popular with the *Hermes* crew as Charles had been during his naval training and it was said, more than once, that he was 'very conscious of being royal'. It was one of several times in his life when he seemed intent on 'pulling rank' and it may have been because he found the transition from prince to pilot very demanding.

'Of course I like being a prince,' he once told a reporter, 'but then I've never been anything else.'

Now he was first and foremost a sailor. The prince must take second place to the midshipman and, for the first time in his life, he had no personal detective until the ship docked and he met him at the end of the gangway.

'If only he could forget that his mother is the Queen once in a while,' a colleague complained. It seemed he did forget when he and a few shipmates

Royal Parachute brothers, Prince Charles and Prince Andrew enjoy a joke with their RAF colleagues during their parachute training course.

Prince Andrew at twenty-one in his formal uniform as Midshipman in the Royal Navy. His decorations are, left, the CVO (Commander of the Royal Victorian Order), and right, the Jubilee medal.

dropped into Trader Jon's Bar Pigalle in Pensicola, famous for its topless girls and military souvenirs. The newspaper photographs show Andrew equally interested in both.

Back in England he wore the green beret of the Royal Marine Commandos when he went with his intake to RAF Leeming in Yorkshire for basic flying training on Bulldog aircraft. He completed the course two weeks ahead of schedule. Then came a long period of arduous training flying helicopters at the Royal Naval Air Station at Culdrose in Cornwall.

He graduated from a light single-engined Gazelle to a Sea King used on anti-submarine warfare. Then to a troop-carrying assault helicopter, the Wessex V. As part of an intensive air crew survival course, it was overturned

Prince Andrew on parade at Dartmouth, aged 20, at the start of his naval career.

Prince Andrew relaxing in tropical uniform when H.M.S. Invincible called at Barbados for 10 days.

in a water tank, twenty feet deep so that pilots could practise escaping from it and swim to the surface. Other courses covered fire-fighting and the basic theories of nuclear warfare.

Andrew celebrated his twenty-first birthday there with 'chips with everything' in the wardroom mess during the day's routine. But his best birthday gift came soon afterwards, in April 1981, when his father, wearing the uniform of an Admiral of the Fleet, presented him with his pilot's wings and the Louis Newmark Trophy for the highest flying marks on the course.

The postponed birthday party was held at Windsor Castle in the summer

Prince Andrew plays 'Action Man'.
Andrew suspended in a mock parachute
during training.

Prince Andrew with a fellow crew
member beside the 'Brazen Hussey', as
the helicopter was affectionately known
on board HMS *Brazen*.

Prince Andrew in the Falklands. The twenty-two year old prince saw a great deal of action in the South Atlantic. He is seen here being interviewed on the steps of Government House in Port Stanley after the re-taking of the islands by the British. He was involved in several rescue missions from his carrier ship, the *Invincible*, and when the *Atlantic Conveyor* was hit by Exocet missiles, he was one of the pilots who went overhead to drop lines to survivors in the sea or in liferafts before winching them to safety and finally landing them on HMS *Hermes*.

Prince Andrew in the pilot's seat of a Fleet Air Arm Gazelle training helicopter. The squadron badge on his sleeve indicates he has undergone a course in parachuting.

and the guns saluted a double celebration by a twenty-one-year-old fully fledged naval helicopter pilot ready to be posted to an operational squadron.

In October 1981 he joined 820 Sea King Squadron on the carrier HMS *Invincible*, a peacetime anti-submarine warfare support carrier to NATO. He was one of 107 officers in a company of 903 strong and, apart from flying duties, had, like the other officers, executive responsibilities within the squadron. He was, as was emphasised in training, a naval officer first and a pilot second. He was known as 'H' (for Highness) and, apart from flying duties as an Assistant Divisional Officer, he shared responsibility for running a group of fifteen squadron handlers and airmen, and took care of his men's training, their welfare and progress.

He was one of two pilots who, with an observer and aircrewman, made up

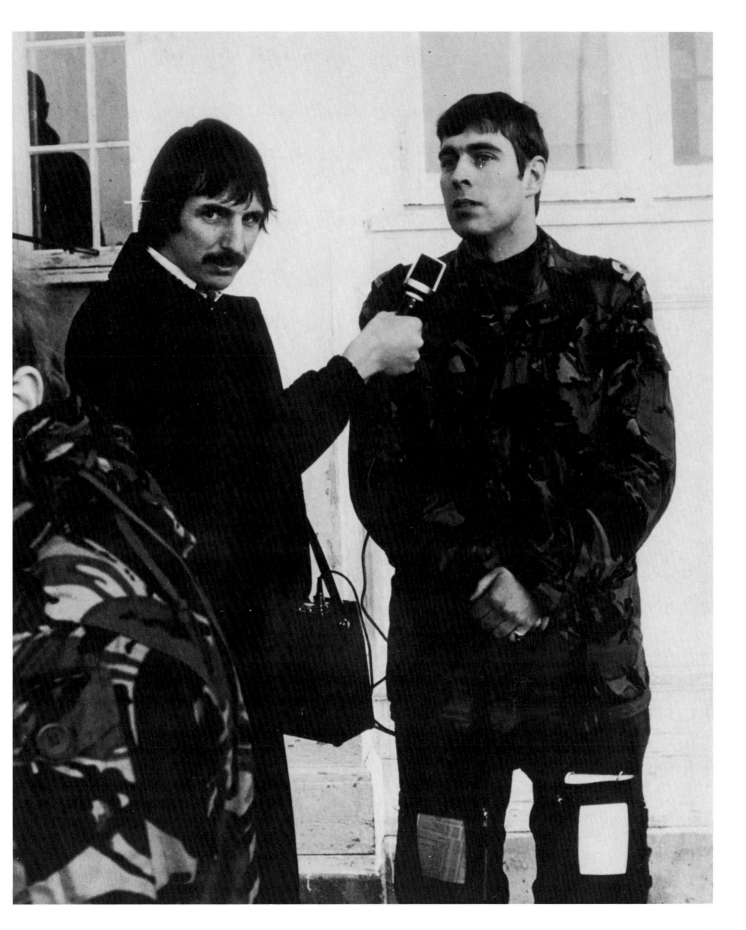

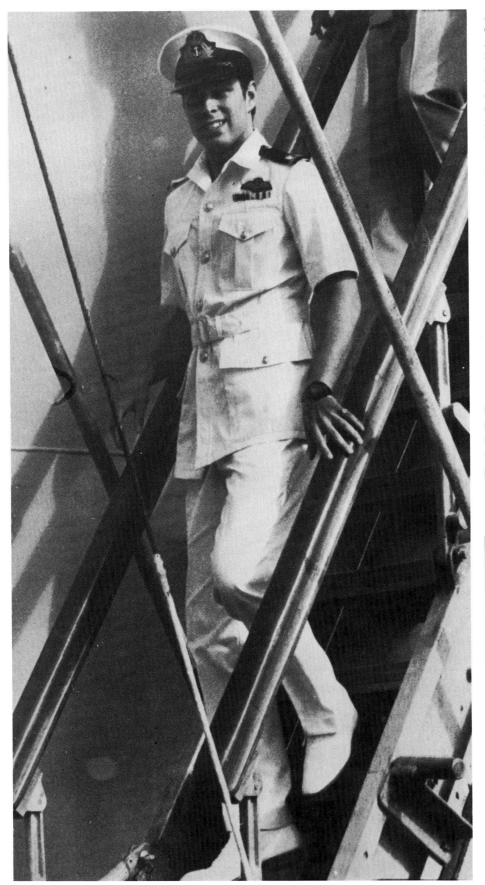

An Officer and a Gentleman. Looking every inch the dashing young prince, Andrew steps ashore in Barbados from HMS *Invincible*, 1983. Prince Andrew and his shipmates stayed on the Caribbean holiday island for ten days, during which time they attended a series of official functions, beginning with a reception hosted by Governor-General Sir Deighton Ward.

Prince Andrew relaxing on board HMS *Invincible* in Barbados.

A Triumphant Return. Prince Andrew in exuberant mood after his return from the Falklands aboard HMS *Invincible*. The entire ship's company were welcomed by a huge, cheering crowd of families and friends as well as thousands of wellwishers, not to mention the band of the Royal Marines.

one of fourteen flying crews who worked in rotation on anti-submarine tactics in the North Altantic. When on duty, he and his crew attended an initial briefing and then turned up on the flight deck about half an hour before take-off. A sortie might take them up to four hours and, on return, it was back to the briefing room, followed by a period of unwinding after the hours of intense concentration on the small radar screen which was virtually all the crew could see when they were in the air.

Andrew had his own cabin and his social life centred round the wardroom and home-made entertainment. There he indulged his pleasant malicious sense of humour and his boyhood tendency to tell risqué jokes which he often found so hilarious that he fell about, helpless with laughter.

For exercise there was fencing, badminton and deck hockey in the hangar. The ship's complement included Chinese launderymen to whiten the official whites, Chinese tailors who produced made-to-measure suits in record time and Chinese cobblers who made sandals for under £8.00 a pair. There was also a gift shop and radio and television stations for light entertainment.

All such refinements disappeared in March 1982 when reports came that a number of Argentinians had sailed to the Falkland Islands to collect scrap metal from a disused whaling station and then hoisted their country's flag. On 2nd April, the British Foreign Secretary, Lord Carrington, confirmed that Argentina had invaded and captured the Islands in an air and sea operation.

Portrait of a pilot. Prince Andrew as a Fleet Air Arm helicopter pilot attached to HMS *Invincible*. Behind him is a Royal Navy Lynx helicopter.

Prince Andrew shares a joke at a tree planting ceremony with the Queen and Prince Philip.

A smiling Prince Andrew chatting with shipmates on H.M.S. Invincible. In the background is his Sea King helicopter.

The British Government immediately ordered a Task Force to go to the islanders' aid and, three days later, the fleet set sail from Portsmouth, led by the aircraft carriers *Hermes* and *Invincible*. On board *Invincible* was a sub-lieutenant who was second in line to the British throne. It never occurred to him that he would not take part if it came to fighting.

His Commanding Officer, Lieutenant-Commander Ralph Wykes-Sneyd, confirmed he would order him into battle just as he would anyone else in the squadron.

The task of the Sea King helicopters during the Falklands campaign was to

Welcome to HMS *Brazen*. Prince Andrew is greeted on his arrival to take up duty on his new warship, HMS *Brazen*. The helicopter is affectionately known as 'The Brazen Hussey', and Prince Andrew persuaded beautiful television presenter Selina Scott to autograph a section of the fuselage when he appeared as a guest on her show. He also forced her to add a kiss for each member of the helicopter crew!

check that the waters ahead of the fleet were free from submarines by taking sonar readings, fetch and carry men and supplies, conduct search and rescue missions in freezing stormy conditions and act as decoys for deadly Exocet missiles.

To keep the men, their machines and techniques at maximum efficiency during peacetime, *Invincible* had taken part in exercises with allied navies to demonstrate to the powers-that-be that they were a force to be reckoned with. When the great carrier entered a foreign port with full ceremony, officers and crew were lined up and aircraft parked on deck. The publicity was well worthwhile.

When the officers lined up dressed in their whites, it was often remarked that only one or two of them carried ceremonial swords. This was because swords were optional as, with leather scabbards, they cost nearly £600 each.

The Sea King Mark V anti-submarine helicopter carried four torpedoes and four depth charges and its most dangerous operation was to act as a decoy target and lure the devastating radar-directed Exocet missiles away from *Invincible*. It did so by hovering near the carrier to present a large low radar target. Because Exocet theoretically travelled low over the sea and was supposed not to be able to rise higher than twenty-seven feet, as soon as it was seen to be travelling straight towards the helicopter the plane quickly gained height and the missile passed harmlessly underneath it. Nevertheless, when *Sheffield* was hit the Exocet missile was seen by many, including

A royal welcome. Prince Andrew bends to kiss his grandmother, the Queen Mother, on the cheek. The royal party called at Scrabster during the cruise which preceded their annual holiday at Balmoral.

Prince Andrew, to fly over the ship's mast well over twenty-seven feet high!

Andrew was hovering over *Invincible* when he saw *Sheffield* explode under a direct hit.

'For the first ten minutes we really didn't know which way to turn and what to do,' he said. 'I knew where I was and I was fairly frightened.'

There was also the danger of being hit by mistake by missiles from his own ship or by others from the Task Force when they fired at attacking aircraft. Three times he felt British Sea Wolf missiles pass uncomfortably close.

'It really makes the hair stand up on the back of your neck,' he admitted. 'It is not much fun having one of those fellows pick you out as a target.'

He added that his most daunting moment of the war came when he was helping to ferry the wounded from the stricken container ship *Atlantic Conveyor*, hit by an Exocet missile which had narrowly missed *Invincible*. Andrew co-piloted his helicopter and helped to pluck many men from the icy waters. The rescue of those survivors has been described as one of the most heroic episodes of the war.

Prince Andrew laying a wreath for the Falklands dead at the Cenotaph.

Seaman Michael Chapman told how the helicopter passed overhead, dropped a line and picked up three men from the raft and three from the sea.

'I was winched up and clambered into the helicopter to find Prince Andrew at the control. He asked if there were any more down there. I said "yes" and he held position.... He was very cool, just like the rest of the crew. It would be nice if I could buy him a pint to say "thanks" one day.'

Prince Andrew was airborne when the *Atlantic Conveyor* was hit. He said 'I saw it being struck by the missile, and it was something I will never forget. It was horrific. At the same time I saw a 4.5mm shell come quite close to us and I saw my ship *Invincible* firing her missiles. Normally I would say it was spectacular, but at the time it was my most frightening moment of the war.'

The squadron spent many flying hours on search and rescue missions and load-lifting and troop-lifting as well as fulfilling its primary role of anti-submarine fighting.

Speaking of Andrew, long after the campaign was over his commanding officer Commander Ralph Wykes-Sneyd, said:

Prince Andrew leaning forward to kiss his grandmother, the Queen Mother, when the Royal Yacht Britannia called at Scrabster during a cruise which took the Royal Family to Scotland for their annual holiday at Balmoral.

'He was a very capable young man; an above average pilot; professional and very sound. There were about fifty officers in the squadron and he got on very well with them all. They were an extrovert bunch and he mixed in very well. You may have blue blood but the 'Royal' tag doesn't rate much mustard – particularly in the air. He wouldn't have wanted it anyway.

'There were fourteen crews flying twenty-four hours a day, seven days a week for the whole conflict and he took his turn. He was the youngest officer in the squadron and comparatively inexperienced. He certainly enjoyed the odd practical joke – particularly when the press were around. He told them his favourite occupation was billiards and that there was a table down in the bilge of the ship – which of course was quite untrue.'

When Argentina surrendered Andrew telephoned his mother from a satellite telephone link.

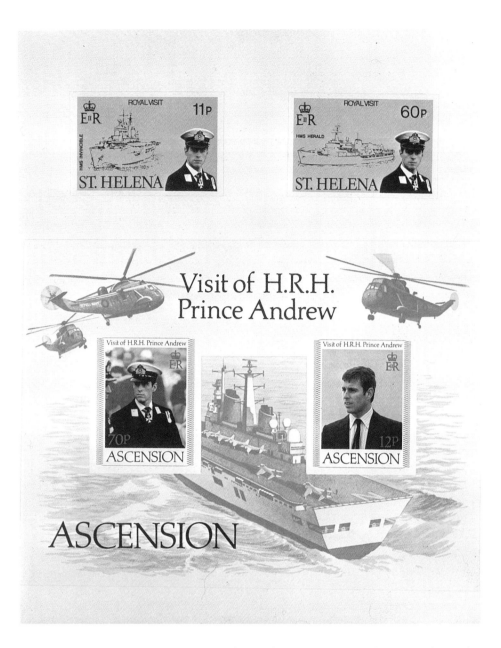

Prince Andrew on stamps commemorating his visit to Ascension Island.

'I made the call and she was in,' he told reporters, naively. 'It is about the right time of the evening. She was quite surprised to hear my voice.'

Tales about Andrew's heroism are legion and it was as if few people remembered that, historically, princes always went to war, on horseback if not in helicopters.

A Welsh guardsman told how the prince landed his helicopter only feet away from an Argentine minefield when ferrying troops to a battlefield just before the ceasefire. 'He knew the risk he was taking and gave the thumbs-up sign after touching down on a narrow road three feet from the nearest mine,' he said.

Andrew was endearingly frank about his fears:

'When there was fear,' he said 'I overcame it with the simple maxim that I must think positive. I told myself I'm going to survive this.'

But the war had changed him, he said, because of the loneliness he had experienced.

'That is the one thing that stands out,' he told reporters, 'and it is never more lonely than when you are lying down on the deck with missiles flying around and you are on your own.'

Other changes were in store. When he heard that Prince William was born Andrew yelled with excitement and ordered drinks all round. A friend asked why he was so delighted since the new prince had demoted him to third in the line of succession, Andrew roared with laughter.

'That's exactly why,' he said 'Now I'll be able to have more privacy.'

There was to be no privacy for him in liberated Port Stanley where wherever he went, he was beseiged by girls asking for autographs. Nevertheless, he pronounced it 'quite a nice little town – the perfect place to spend my honeymoon'.

Before then he would be back to the island with which his name will always be associated. Meanwhile, he and his companions returned to a heroes' welcome at Portsmouth. The Queen, Prince Philip and Princess Anne did not wait to meet him there but went by Royal barge to board *Invincible* at Spithead.

He was bubbling over with excitement when the ship docked at Portsmouth, appropriately overlooked by Nelson's *Victory*. He had been away for 166 days and had been refused permission to fly home for Prince William's christening. He marched down the gang plank gripping in his teeth a red rose presented by a ten-year-old school girl, but it did not hide his grin.

A red rose in fact was presented to every sailor from *Invincible*, *Canberra*, the *Q.E.2* and the *Hermes* and a bouquet of them for the Queen, given by a jubilant Croydon florist.

Prince Andrew even greeted the press party like long-lost friends.

'I am obviously looking forward to going home,' he said 'but not to be going to being a prince.'

He had a month's leave before joining 702 Naval Air Squadron at Portland, Dorset, for a six-month course on Lynx helicopters. He completed his hundred flying hours and joined the 3,500 ton frigate *Brazen* as their only pilot. He was also promoted to Lieutenant and appointed a personal ADC to the Queen.

HMS *Brazen* patrolled the bleak waters around the Falklands and Prince Andrew, in his small Lynx helicopter, watched for Argentine planes. There were none. He grew a beard while, in his own words, he spent three months looking 'at the back end of ships and around fishing boats'.

Towards the end of that South Atlantic tour with *Brazen* he was invited to open the Falklands' new £400-million international airport at Port Stanley. The ceremony was to be attended by the British Defence Secretary, Michael Heseltine, and a group of VIPs who would make the eighteen-hour flight from Brize Norton, Oxfordshire, in a TriStar for what was to be the aircraft's inaugural flight. The new airport would be closed to all air traffic until the inaugural flight had landed.

Reporter Michael Nicholson was covering the event for ITN and he and Prince Andrew knew each other from the time when Nicholson reported the East African tour made by the Queen, Prince Philip and Prince Andrew in 1978.

'The Royals were driving through Malawi in a beautiful open red Rolls,' Nicholson recalled. 'Just as they drove past us our camera jammed and we missed a marvellous shot. I was determined to get it and the cameraman and

Prince Andrew
leaving St. Pauls after
the Falklands
Memorial Service,
with the Princess of
Wales in the
background.

Prince Andrew sharing a joke amidst a happy crowd at Culdrose Air Base.

Prince Andrew joking with shipmates on HMS *Invincible* after the Falklands conflict.

I ran like mad to try and catch up with them, until I stumbled and fell and broke my arm.

The next time I met Prince Andrew was on HMS *Invincible* when I was going out to cover the Falklands campaign. As soon as he saw me he shouted out, "Hey! How's that arm?" and it was four years since I'd seen him!

As well as that fantastic memory he had a knack of knowing everything that was going on. For instance, one day, I decided to take the day off and walk over the island. There was not a plane in sight but the next morning he said to me, "Hey! What were you doing deer-stalking across Falkland?"

I was there to report the opening of the Mount Pleasant airport and, while we were waiting for the VIP plane to arrive, Prince Andrew took some of us

HMS *Invincible* returns from the Falklands to a tumultuous welcome at Portsmouth.

up in his Lynx helicopter to give us an aerial press preview. He was a superb pilot and a daring and adventurous one – you wouldn't find anyone to argue with that!

He knew perfectly well no one was allowed to use the airport until the VIPs arrived and he had performed the opening ceremony but, as we looked down from the air, he just couldn't resist the chance of being the first pilot to use the new runway and, for some reason, everyone in the control tower seemed to turn a blind eye.

"Hey!" he shouted gleefully as we touched down, "I'm the first lad to land!"'

# The Playboy Prince

Two weeks after his return from the Falklands war, Andrew had flown off on a well-deserved holiday to the West Indies amid an outburst of hysterical indignation at his choice of travelling companion. She was an old friend, American-born actress Kathleen Dee-Anne Stark, known as Koo, the only daughter of Wilbur Stark, an American film producer, and his former wife Mrs Kathleen Caruso, who had once acted on television under the name of Kathi Norris.

Koo was three years older than Andrew, and they had met in February

1982 after she had broken off her engagement to a millionaire advertising executive, Robert Winsor. There had been instant mutual attraction. They were often seen at London's smartest night-clubs and friends said they seemed to be very much in love.

While Andrew was fighting in the Falklands, however, an episode in Koo's life was unearthed which put a completely different complexion on the romance: it was revealed that she had appeared completely naked in a mildly erotic film, *The Awakening of Emily*, produced by the Earl of Pembroke, who, it so happened, is related to both the Princess of Wales and Sarah Ferguson. He is fourth cousin to them both through their mutual descendancy from the 1st Duke of Abercorn. Apparently the BBC considered the romance between Koo and Andrew potentially significant enough to

Carolyn Seaward, an early target for the Prince's affections. This photograph was taken in 1982 which was the year in which he became involved in the Falklands action and in which his elder brother Prince Charles became a father for the first time.

Badminton Horse Trials, 1976. Prince Andrew in the company of the attractive Duchess of Roxburghe (formerly Lady Jane Grosvenor whose sister is married to Lord Lichfield). It was at the Duke and Duchess of Roxburghe's beautiful home, Floors Castle, that Prince Andrew proposed to Sarah Ferguson.

Prince Andrew and King Constantine of Greece at a clay pigeon shoot.

show an excerpt from the film on the nine o'clock news. The Palace was silent, but in September 1982 Koo was a guest at Balmoral. On Andrew's return from the war the press were waiting with sharpened pencils for the next instalment. They got it.

Prince Andrew and Koo Stark, travelling under the name of Mr and Mrs Cambridge, took an economy-class flight, paid for by the Queen, to the Caribbean island of Mustique. It was the signal for a moral outbreak of press verbiage interspersed with titillating trifles that left the readers reeling.

The *Sun* devoted its centre spread to stills from 'sizzling sex films' featuring Koo; the *Mirror* had an interview with Koo's cleaning lady who

Prince Andrew crewing on one of the challenge yachts in trials for the Americas Cup in 1983.

Prince Andrew on board the support launch for the British Challenger, *Victory*, in the Americas Cup in 1983.

Andrew's Birthday Date. Prince Andrew began his 24th birthday celebrations with Carolyn Herbert, the 21-year-old daughter of the Queen's racing manager Lord Porchester. They went to the Royal Opera House, Covent Garden.

Prince Andrew Goes To Hollywood. Andrew may not have endeared himself to the press during his visit to America, but the British film stars who helped organise his fund-raising trip were delighted with his performance. So much so that in response to general criticism of the Prince's behaviour — in particular the paint-spraying episode when Andrew doused photographers in white paint — that they banded together to write a letter of thanks to the 24-year-old Prince. Michael Caine said: 'He gave this trip 101% of his efforts. He wore himself out for us and did a lot more than he needed to have done. He's a kind-hearted gentleman, not a badly behaved brat.'

Prince Andrew in Mustique in October 1982. Unfortunately he was so hounded by the press that he was forced to cut short his stay and return to Britain.

said she had seen the prince leaving Koo's flat in the mornings 'always looking rather tired'; and the *Daily Mail* reported that the couple were being chaperoned on their holiday by Koo's mother:

'My wife is with them under express orders from the Queen,' said Koo's well-meaning stepfather, Carl Caruso, in an unlikely statement that was promptly denied by the Palace.

Not to be outdone, Wilbur Stark announced: 'My daughter's a fantastic girl – she doesn't drink she's not flashy, she doesn't use make-up to excess, she dresses very carefully.... She is also most discreet. The prince is a very lucky guy.'

The world's press took up the story. It exceeded belief when it was known that three journalists were in the royal party, including an American reporter, who hoped to sell her account of the happenings on Mustique for a reputed £150,000. Palace security staff were blamed for not checking the identities of Andrew's travelling companions.

'Andrew Ordered Home' read the *Sun's* headline, a week after the holiday had begun. He flew home under the name of Mr Newman while Miss Stark departed in another aircraft for Miami.

It was left to the loyal young Prince Edward to express the unofficial royal viewpoint.

Prince Andrew enjoying a joke with TV personality, Jenny Handley, during a celebrity clay-pigeon shooting competition.

'He came back from that holiday more drawn, more tired, than he had from three months at war,' he said. 'I think to treat someone who's just come back from serving his country like that is absolutely despicable.'

His reaction was backed by an invitation to Koo from the Queen to join the family at Balmoral the following summer. Perhaps it was a reward for her discreet silence about the whole affair. By the end of the year, however, the romance was over. Koo turned to photography and produced an excellent book, *Stark Contrasts*. While she was working on it she met Timothy Jeffries, the twenty-two-year-old heir to the £50-million Green Shield Stamp fortune built up by his grandfather. They married in August 1984 but separated sixteen months later.

When Koo learned of Andrew's engagement to Sarah Ferguson, she was totally shattered and distressed, according to her close girlfriend who, coincidentally, had been at school with Sarah. Koo felt a complete failure after her own marriage had broken up, her friend said.

Prince Andrew's susceptibility to beautiful girls started during his Gordonstoun days with 'Andrew's Harem', Sue Barnard, a vivacious young American; Clio Nathaniels, an architect's daughter from Nassau; and Kirsty Richmond, the daughter of a widowed nurse.

For a long time Clio Nathaniels seemed the firm favourite, particularly when she was invited to Windsor Castle for the weekend. Then she suddenly left Gordonstoun and returned to Nassau after rumours of a lovers' quarrel which the school authorities firmly denied.

She was replaced by Kirsty Richmond from Suffolk, who was invited to Sandringham for the New Year, to Balmoral for a week in the summer, and to spend a night at Buckingham Palace on her way back to school, to make it easier for her to catch the early-morning train to Inverness. She shared Andrew's enthusiasm for ski-ing, tennis and pottery but, a Buckingham Palace spokesman emphasised, she was 'just a school friend'.

Prince Andrew clutching his prize at the end of a celebrity clay-pigeon shooting competition organised by ex-world champion racing driver, Jackie Stewart, who is a godfather to Peter, the eldest of Captain Mark Phillips' and Princess Anne's children.

Prince Andrew resting beside Lord Lichfield during a clay-pigeon shooting competition.

Royal Horseplay. Prince Charles and Andrew share a private joke during a lull between the action at a polo match. This photograph shows the obvious affinity between these royal brothers and their shared sense of fun.

The list of his girlfriends was endless. It included Finola Hughes, the actress and dancer; Clare Park, a model who advertised Oil of Ulay and Ryvita on television commercials; the Hon. Carolyn Herbert, daughter of Lord Porchester, the Queen's racing manager; baronet's daughter Vicki Hodge, a model who strolled on to *Invincible* and led the prince to a beach party with assorted topless girlfriends; Kim Deas, a cover girl; and Katie Rabett, a gynaecologist's daughter and model.

In America it was the same story, and the Prince who was too good-looking for his own good, 'the Robert Redford of the family' as Charles described him, left a trail of would-be girlfriends after attending the

A day at Rhode Island spent in typical British fashion. Prince Andrew watched a game of cricket at Beachwood Manor surrounded by beautiful women including Lana Paton, girlfriend of Peter De Savary, head of the British challenge for the Americas Cup in 1983 (right), and Suzy Pearce, of the British Information Office (left).

1983 Americas Cup ball at Newport, Rhode Island. On that trip he also found time to visit his old Canadian school, Lakefield College.

They mobbed him like a pop star in St Helena in 1984 when he represented the Queen at the 150th anniversary of the island's annexation as a British colony. He could hardly suppress his grin when the governor who greeted him at Jamiestown missed his footing and fell into the sea.

That grin proved his downfall again later that year, when his first solo fund-raising trip abroad turned into something of a disaster. The four-day tour was to raise money for British Olympic and Gordonstoun Associations. The trouble started at a ball in Los Angeles when his dancing partner, Wendy

Allen, a Gordonstoun old girl, became distraught at the excessive press attention, lost her head and dashed into an elevator shouting 'leave me alone'.

Perhaps Andrew sympathised with her feelings. The next day, whilst visiting a housing rehabilitation project in the black ghetto district of Watts, he was shown a new type of paint-spraying gun. He examined it, and, either accidentally or deliberately, turned it on the watching cameramen, spraying them and their cameras with white paint.

'I enjoyed that,' he was reported to have said, grinning mischievously, or with bravado. Unfortunately, no one else shared his enjoyment. The English and American cameramen estimated the damage to their equipment at £15,000 which Buckingham Palace promptly offered to pay. However, they never disclosed whether the money came from the Prince's own salary as a Royal Naval Lieutenant (about £10,500 per annum), from the Queen, his insurers, or from his Civil List allowance of £20,000 a year.

His supporters claimed it was an accident, but he made no attempt to apologise to the victims. That night, at a star-studded banquet and concert arranged by the British Olympic Association, Michael Caine, master of ceremonies, spoke up for Prince Andrew, describing him as the 'Vincent Van Gogh for free-range grafiti', and commended him for helping to raise at least £180,000 for the Olympics.

An amusing photograph of Koo Stark taken in St James' Park with Buckingham Palace in the background.

Prince Andrew's seaside romp. Whilst spending his shore leave on Barbados in 1983 he was hotly pursued by the press because he spent much of his time with three lovely girls who he had met at a party on board HMS *Invincible*. They were ex-model Vicki Hodge (shown in this photograph), 21-year-old Tracy Lamb, and 26-year-old Lucy Wisdom, and they spent much of their time frolicking with Prince Andrew and other friends on the beach – in and out of their swimming costumes!

Katie Rabett was one of Prince Andrew's girlfriends who was hotly tipped to as a 'serious contender' in the Royal marriage stakes, and was the subject of many of his photographs. Here she is seen emerging from her Ealing home with her mother to face the press at the height of the speculation about her relationship with Prince Andrew. According to the photographers, both appeared calm and friendly in the face of such intense media interest.

Prince Andrew TV Star. The Prince emerging from the studios of TV AM following the recording of his first TV interview with David Frost who pronounced Andrew an expert. 'He was so relaxed it was impossible to believe it was his first time.'

But the damage to Andrew's reputation, both in England and America, was considerable, and he returned home, depressed and jet-lagged to such headlines as: 'Clown Prince or Royal Hooligan?' The headline appeared in a newspaper, which eighteen months earlier had hailed him as 'Hero of the Falklands'. Andrew had learnt the first lesson in dealing with the press; that they can put you on a pedestal, but they are even more adept at knocking you off. It is rumoured that after all these indignities, Andrew also got a stern dressing down from Prince Philip, and he must have been left wondering why and how he 'sometimes got it all wrong'.

Later, when being interviewed on the BBC Woman's Hour programme, he said the incident was 'a complete accident and very unfortunate. I think I probably learnt my lesson to point the paint in the right direction the next time... towards the wall, which is in fact what I did, but by that time it was too late.'

The Prince, who is a pilot, and idolised by women to an embarrassing degree, has had so many lessons to learn. Some are apparent in his first published album of photographs called simply *Photographs by* HRH *the Prince Andrew*. He described this book as 'a small slice of autobiography, recording memories and impressions'. As such, the sensitive photographs and his honest comments about their background tell part of his story.

The photograph of his helicopter parked on the lawn at Balmoral while

The photographer Prince. Andrew emerges from a London studio clutching a portfolio of his photographs. His love of photography found a creative outlet in the Ilford Calendar and a book of his photographs which were published in 1985. The book won encouraging reviews from the professionals, and this is an interest which Prince Andrew obviously intends pursuing.

Koo Stark – perhaps the most famous and infamous of Prince Andrew's girlfriends – she was disapproved of because, when she was seventeen, she appeared in a soft-porn film, *Emily*, which included a nude shower scene. However, her relationship with Prince Andrew was obviously a serious one and she was visibly upset when it came to an end.

Koo Snaps Back. Like Prince Andrew, Koo Stark is also a keen photographer and frequently turns the tables on the professionals. She has also had a book of her photographs published.

the Queen walks towards the front door, a pack of corgis at her heels, was taken when he and his crew 'dropped in for tea'. It shows the happy blending of his chosen career and his home life.

He has come to terms with the need for security and accepts the way it can be blended into the environment as in the picture of his British policeman, stripped to the waist, knee deep in water, fishing in a Canadian lake. Andrew has also come to terms with his destiny, and enjoys the moments of loneliness which he is sometimes able to enjoy, as in his haunting photographs of the great lakes and skies and mountains in the North-West Territory of Canada. 'Loneliness is a theme of my photography,' he told David Frost in an interview, 'I am a recluse.'

The Sporting Prince. Andrew, his teeth gritted, takes this hockey match with a sporting seriousness which typifies his attitude towards life.

Ghostly Image. Actress Finola Andrews, another of Prince Andrew's favoured lady friends, proved an interesting subject to photograph. She is pictured in a flowing Zhandra Rhodes dress in an eerie picture entitled 'The 9th Wife – Dungeons Windsor' which was featured in the Ilford Calendar in 1985.

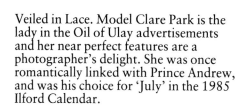

Veiled in Lace. Model Clare Park is the lady in the Oil of Ulay advertisements and her near perfect features are a photographer's delight. She was once romantically linked with Prince Andrew, and was his choice for 'July' in the 1985 Ilford Calendar.

Prince Andrew with the Duke and Duchess of Roxburghe and Princess Margaret and the young Viscount Linley at a point-to-point meeting.

There are evocative studies of beautiful women in his book, including Clare Park, Katie Rabett, and other models, and his indebtedness to Koo Stark is affirmed in his Introduction. She is credited with having led him to this 'newly found means of freedom, and self expression'.

He catches the memories he wants to keep alive, of the things he finds important: the peace and tranquillity of a wood in summer, carpeted with bluebells... quietly sailing around the western isles... the Queen Mother's enchanting Castle of Mey... Balmoral for a few weeks' private holiday and the annual recharging of the royal batteries before the 'silly season'.

This self confessed 'enthusiastic amateur' is not yet a Norman Parkinson or a Lord Lichfield, as the professional critics were only too keen to point out, but there is no denying the fact that Andrew has a creative talent and has found a challenging outlet for it through his photography. As could be said about many things in his life, 'he is learning'. The refreshing thing about Andrew is that he has never been afraid of learning anything.

# A Bride for Andrew

'I'll know there and then if I do find somebody. Then it's going to come like a lightning bolt ...' Prince Andrew said, talking of the likelihood of finding a bride. He was unaware that he had already found one.

Sarah Margaret Ferguson was born on 15th October 1959 at a private nursing home in Welbeck Street, London. She was the younger daughter of Major and Mrs Ronald Ivor Ferguson of Dummer Down House, Hampshire. Her father, a first cousin to Robert Fellows, Deputy Private Secretary to the Queen and now the Prince of Wales's brother-in-law, was the fourth generation of his family to serve in the Life Guards. He commanded the Sovereign's Escort of Household Cavalry and is now Prince Charles's polo manager. He runs the Guards' polo club on the Queen's estate at Windsor. His mother is a first cousin to Princess Alice, Duchess of Gloucester.

Sarah's mother, formerly Susan Mary Wright, also has military connections. Her father, FitzHerbert Wright, former owner of the Butterly Works with a country seat, Yeldersley Hall, was a cavalryman from a distinguished Derbyshire dynasty.

A network of blood and marriage ties has always bound the Royal Family to their courtiers so that Andrew and Sarah were destined to meet in early childhood. An informal photograph shows their two families chatting at Smith's Lawn Polo ground at Windsor. There is the Queen with her corgis, Sarah's long-haired mother looking like a college student in sweater and jeans, Prince Edward chatting to his cousin, Lady Sarah Armstrong Jones and Prince Andrew playing the clown for the benefit of the curly-haired Sarah and her elder sister Jane who were obviously amused by his droll antics.

Sarah, or 'Fergie' as she is known to her friends, was educated at the £485-a-term Danes Hill co-educational prep school in Basingstoke, followed by Hurst Lodge, Sunningdale. The exclusive girls' boarding school, where fees were £1335 a term, put great emphasis on dance and drama and so attracted aspiring actresses and the daughters of theatrical personalities.

Among Sarah's friends were Florence Belmondo, daughter of the French film star Jean Paul Belmondo, Lisa Mulidore, daughter of the dizzy TV blonde Aimi MacDonald. She remembered Fergie surrounded by younger girls who hero-worshipped her. And there was Davida Smart, granddaughter

A sequence of five photographs taken by Lord Lichfield when Sarah Ferguson was three and a half years old.

Ready for anything. Sarah was clearly a fun-loving child and she and Prince Andrew often played together at Windsor – but romance was many years away.

Full of mischief. Not only was Sarah a playmate of Prince Andrew, but she was his equal when it came to childhood pranks.

The gardener's helper. 'I'll never get them all swept up!' Sarah faces a task of Herculean proportions, but looks as though she may still succeed.

An air of determination. Even at the age of three and a half, Sarah was clearly a girl who knew her own mind.

Dwarfed, but not bowed. Sarah is a tiny figure dominated by these huge trees, but her confidence shines through in this early portrait.

A little girl's best friend. At home in her early days, Sarah had security with her cuddly toys; especially Mr Rabbit. Her father kept an extraordinary photograph album which contains many shots of his children's early life, and these photographs have never been seen before, except by close members of the family.

Business as usual the day after the engagement for Sarah Ferguson, who despite the press attention, turned up at the offices of the Mayfair art publishers where she worked. However, there was a marked difference. On this occasion the photographers were kept at bay by the police, and she was accompanied by Prince Andrew's private detective. Life would never be quite the same again!

of the showman Billy Smart who, in the holidays, worked as a trapeze artist.

'Fergie always got things done,' she recalled. 'Not by ordering people about but because she inspired loyalty.' Sarah shared a dormitory with three other girls and was usually the centre of any outbursts of boisterous horse-play like cream bun fights and apple-pie beds, which often occurred. The many young extroverts in the school, anxious to 'do their own thing', frequently created a 'wild atmosphere', according to Alexandra Grant-Adamson, daughter of a diplomatic correspondent for a national newspaper. She remembered being very bored during a maths lesson:

Happy sisters. This enchanting photograph shows Sarah and her sister Jane enjoying a joke together.

Royals aboard. Princess Diana and Prince William, accompanied by Sarah Ferguson, visit Prince Andrew on board HMS *Brazen*. It was this visit in particular which increased speculation about an imminent engagement.

'The window opened out on to a balcony and everyone was throwing pencils, papers and rubbers out of the window,' she said. 'Fergie – I'm sure it was her – actually picked up a whole desk and threw that out as well.'

Like Andrew, the schoolgirl Sarah loved practical jokes.

'She was the gang leader,' a former classmate Susan Clapman recalls. 'She loved midnight feasts in the dorm and I remember one night we all moved our beds into the assembly hall for a laugh.'

Another time, during a PT class, Sarah and her friends smuggled frog-spawn into the changing rooms and filled a girl's pockets with it.

The happy family. Mrs Ronald Ferguson (now Mrs Hector Barrantes) with her two children, Sarah, and (right) Jane, (now Mrs William Makim). Taken in 1967.

Lady Elmhirst, Sarah Ferguson's paternal grandmother, photographed at the wedding of Sarah's sister, Jane, to William Makim in 1976.

Teenage years. Sarah Ferguson as a happy, fun-loving teenager, obviously full of the joys of life.

A military wedding. The wedding took place at St Margaret's, Westminster, of Lieutenant Ronald Ivor Ferguson of the Life Guards – son of Colonel and Mrs A.H. Ferguson of Basingstoke – and Miss Susan Mary Wright, daughter of Mr and the Hon. Mrs FitzHerbert Wright of Grantham. The marriage took place in 1956 and the couple left the church between a Guard of Honour of the Lifeguards.

Mrs Ronald Ferguson, Sarah's stepmother, at a party in London in 1983.

Mr and Mrs William Makim – she is Sarah Ferguson's sister – at their wedding in 1976.

Sarah Ferguson's school, Hurst Lodge.

Sarah Ferguson's childhood home, Dummer Down House, in Hampshire.

The house in Lavender Gardens, Clapham, South London where Sarah lived with Carolyn Beckwith-Smith before she became engaged to Prince Andrew.

During Sarah's second year at Hurst Lodge, however, her mother ran off with the Argentinian polo player, Hector Barrantes, leaving her daughters to the care of their father. Sarah took it the hardest. She was miserable at school, dropped out of the school rounders team and, although she had never been an academic, her work suffered.

She grew closer to her father. At weekends he took her to friends' homes, and to Windsor Safari Park which she loved. Most of all she loved going back to Dummer, to swimming and tennis and the family pony Peanuts. She adored riding and she and Peanuts won a fair share of rosettes at the local gymkhanas.

Whenever her father appeared on the polo field the small red head was

Society portrait. A photograph of Sarah Ferguson's mother taken for *The Tatler*.

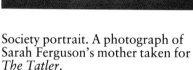

Sarah's father, Major Ronald Ferguson, resting in a hammock between chukkas at a polo match.

usually behind him. Gradually, as their relationship deepened, school was fun again and when her father remarried in 1976 she was ready to accept the Norfolk farmer's daughter, Susan Deptford, as her young stepmother.

By then she had been joint head girl at the school with Fenella Heron, daughter of the comedian Ted Rogers. She gained six 'O' levels in Art, English Language and Literature, Spoken English, French and Biology. On her last night at school, she took the traditional nude dip in the school swimming pool at midnight.

'If there was any fun Sarah would be in the midst of it,' her former headmistress Mrs Celia Merrick recalled. 'From being a very small girl she always had charm, humour and a sense of fun. She had a very sunny disposition ... enormously cheerful, bubbly and fun-loving. But she was not a superficial girl and had a stubborn streak. I should think she will suit the young prince very well – she is a strong enough character to keep him in order!'

These characteristics show in her handwriting. A handwriting expert, Jenny Halfon, shown a specimen of it anonymously, said it represented 'a very bubbly person with a great sense of humour. A real character, in fact. She's a hard taskmaster who expects and demands perfection from others and if she doesn't get it becomes very annoyed. She is outspoken, hot-tempered and could be a right bossy-boots.

However there is a lot of niceness about her. She is very kind-hearted, caring and protective towards herself and her family.'

After school Sarah took a course in shorthand, typing and book-keeping at Queen's Secretarial College, London, where she and her best friend there, Charlotte Eden, daughter of Sir John Eden, now Lord Eden of Wintun, shared the distinction of both being bottom of the class.

'Fergie is very intelligent,' Charlotte said, 'but like me she was never cut out to be a secretary. We were at the college because we knew it was important to get some sort of training and we both managed to scrape

Sarah's stepmother, Susan Ferguson, celebrating outside their home in Dummer, Hampshire, following the announcement of the royal engagement.

The first boyfriend. Mr Kim Smith-Bingham, Sarah Ferguson's first serious boyfriend, photographed in July 1978. They first met while Sarah was staying with her mother and stepfather in Argentina. They became friends and met up again in London in 1980, although they never lived together as he spent most of his time in Verbier where he ran a ski equipment company.

A polo duo. Mr and Mrs Hector Barrantes at a polo match at Windsor in July 1976. Unfortunately Mr Barrantes' Argentinian nationality caused a severe strain on their relationship with their British friends during the Falklands conflict, especially because of his international reputation as a polo player.

Village locals. Major Ronald Ferguson and Sarah leaving the village shop in Dummer, Hampshire.

Player and manager. Prince Charles and his polo manager Major Ronald Ferguson discussing the finer points of the game during a meeting at Windsor in 1984.

Nightclub gossip. Sarah Ferguson with her friend Mrs George Morton at the Hippodrome nightclub, one of Prince Andrew's favourite haunts.

A night out on the town. Sarah Ferguson arriving for the Marquis of Blandford's birthday party in 1984. She is an old friend of Jamie Blandford whose tragic addiction to drugs has caused both his family and friends a great deal of heartache over the past few years.

99

Beach beauty! Sarah Ferguson, aged four years and nine months showing great style in front of the camera.

The greatest of friends. Princess Diana and Sarah Ferguson talking animatedly at a polo match at Windsor.

Prince Andrew and Sarah Ferguson enjoying each others company at Royal Ascot in 1985 at the beginning of their romance.

A photograph taken by an observant cameraman of Princess Diana and Sarah Ferguson watching a polo match at Cowdray Park in Sussex.

through the course. Money was very tight. Fergie was likely to rush to a corner cafe for a takeaway hamburger.'

When she left the secretarial college after her nine months' course, the assessment typed on the student's index card described her as a 'bright, bouncy redhead. A bit slapdash, but has initiative and personality which she will well use to her advantage when she gets older and accepts responsibility happily.'

She was not ready for responsibility and took a cookery course before getting her first job as a secretary with a Knightsbridge public relations company, Durden-Smith Communications (owned by Neil Durden-Smith, the husband of the TV presenter Judith Chalmers). Her boss, Peter Cunard, admired her guts. 'She was never afraid of anyone,' he said, but he was annoyed by the time she wasted on the telephone arranging her social engagements.

She left after three years to go with her friend Charlotte on an adventurous 6000-mile journey from Argentina to the USA, starting from her mother's home near Buenos Aires where they spent Christmas.

'It was a lovely Christmas,' Charlotte said, 'Sarah gets on well with her stepfather. There is no question of her being embarrassed about him being an Argentinian or not wanting him to be at the marriage.'

An old flame. Sarah Ferguson and 48-year-old racing manager Paddy McNally were almost inseparable for two and a half years, until the summer of 1985. They first met during the Racing World Championships in 1976 after he became a widower; and Sarah became 'best friends' with his two children Sean and Rollo who are both at Stonyhurst, the Roman Catholic public school. The relationship came to an end in the summer of 1985 after Sarah is alleged to have given him an ultimatum to marry her or separate.

Prince Charles and the 'other woman' in his life. Charles and Sarah Ferguson greeted each other with a friendly kiss when they met at a polo match in 1982.

That Christmas Sarah met her first boyfriend, Kim Smith-Bingham, an old Etonian who was doing a six-months' ranching job. They were to meet up again in London three years later. By that time he was running a ski equipment business in Verbier and Sarah would go there for a month and ski every day.

'She's very good, black run standard,' he said. 'In the evenings we'd go out to restaurants, see friends. She spoke French when necessary and mixed with the large international crowd there. It was great fun. I wasn't especially affluent, probably earning a bit more than my counterparts in England – certainly more than the £5000 a year it was said you needed to live in London.

In the summer I'd spend time in England to be with Fergie and, of course, my family. In England she loved the theatre and cinema, theatre probably the best, especially lightish things like *Barnum*. Afterwards we'd go out to dinner in either her car or mine. I usually paid although after we'd been going out for three years we occasionally went Dutch. She loved giving small dinner parties and sometimes I'd cook her my own speciality, spaghetti bolognese.

If it's true, as people say, that redheads have a terrible temper, then Sarah was not a typical redhead.

We never lived together as the papers said but we did spend a lot of time together. When we split up it was just a question of starting to live different lifestyles.'

After her first meeting with Kim Smith-Bingham in Argentina Sarah and Charlotte left on their 'great adventure', travelling through Argentina and Brazil by bus, sleeping wherever they could and living on a diet of burgers. The old buses bumped over rough roads and for days on end they had no chance to change their clothes. Their fellow travellers were often poor farmers carrying their chickens to market.

Royal and loyal friends. Princess Diana and Sarah Ferguson discuss future prospects at a polo match in the summer of 1982. No one in the royal family is more delighted at Sarah's engagement to Prince Andrew than Diana, and the two are old friends with similar tastes and backgrounds.

An Ascot couple. This was the first inkling that there was a real romance in the air between Prince Andrew and Sarah Ferguson, or 'Fergie' as she became affectionately known. They were together at Ascot for the Royal Meeting in 1975 after Andrew's return from five months at sea on board HMS *Brazen* in the South Atlantic. It was at about the same time this photograph was taken that Sarah is said to have ended her romance with Paddy McNally. However, when questioned about a possible romance between Prince Andrew and Sarah Ferguson, a friend said, 'They are just good friends!'

In the United States they also existed on a tight budget.

'They were carefree, crazy days,' Charlotte said. 'Fergie will remember them as some of the happiest of her life.'

Back in London she worked for a flat-letting agency, and then for an art dealer, William Drummond, who admired her tremendous speed, energy and enthusiasm.

She enjoyed the art world and left Mr Drummond to work for a small Swiss printing company, BCK Graphic Arts, in St George Street, W1, where she liaised with authors and photographers to produce art books and catalogues.

She shared a house in Clapham with Carolyn Beckwith-Smith, whose cousins are Anne Beckwith-Smith, Lady-in-Waiting to the Princess of Wales, and Mrs David Napier, a Lady-in-Waiting to the Duchess of Kent.

The Princess of Wales wanted Sarah as her Lady-in-Waiting but the Palace decided she was too inexperienced, and meanwhile Sarah had formed another romantic attachment. It was to a much older man, Paddy McNally, a widower with two sons at school at Stonyhurst. He was the former manager of the world champion racing-driver Nikki Lauda. Sarah and McNally were involved for about three years, but their relationship ended in 1985 when Sarah realised McNally had no intention of remarrying however much he admired her.

'She was a girl in a million,' he said, 'and anybody would be lucky to go out with her, let alone marry her.'

Sarah's relationship with Paddy McNally, like her romance with Kim Smith-Bingham was a perfect grounding for her forthcoming marriage, according to her 'wicked stepmother', as Sarah affectionately calls Susan Ferguson, now the mother of three young children.

'She never lived with either of them,' Susan said. 'Both relationships were

## HEAD GIRLS

| | | | |
|---|---|---|---|
| 1973 | VICKY JACOB | 1984 | SUZANNE EVANS |
| 1974 | ALEXA LAURISTON | | DAPO ENEFENI |
| | SARAH McCALL | 1985 | FRANCES HOUSTON |
| 1975 | ALEXANDRA BACK | | GEMMA KNIGHT |
| | FELICITY DEAN | 1986 | GILLIAN MURDOCH |
| 1976 | SARAH FERGUSON | | |
| | FENELLA RODGERS | | |
| 1977 | SARAH BUTLER | | |
| | GAIL HADDON | | |
| 1978 | CAROL PHILLIPS-JONES | | |
| | AMANDA NUNN | | |
| 1979 | AMANDA CHAPMAN | | |
| | BELINDA GOLD-BLYTH | | |

A glamorous duo. Princess Diana and Sarah Ferguson watching the prize-giving at the end of a polo match at Windsor.

Sarah Ferguson's name on the list of head girls at her old school, Hurst Lodge.

Shared secrets. A pregnant Princess Diana chatting with Sarah Ferguson at a polo match at Smith's lawn, Windsor.

Spot the royals. In this crowded scene from Royal Ascot in 1985 it is possible to pick out Princess Diana and Prince Andrew, with Sarah Ferguson just visible over his left shoulder.

always terribly tricky – full of goodbyes – so Sarah is well used to 'getting on with it' on her own.

Of course if won't be easy when Andrew goes off on long naval tours but Sarah is determined to keep on working – and I think she'll cope very well.'

Helping her to cope will certainly be the Princess of Wales who, it is generally believed, masterminded the romance.

The present engagement is a triumph for her according to the biographer Hugo Vickers, author of *Debrett's Book of the Royal Wedding*. He writes:

'"Fergie" is one of her closest friends, so now she has an ally at court. "Fergie" is not as pretty as the Princess of Wales, nor does she seem to engage our desire to protect her in the same way. Her self-assurance is in marked contrast to the princess's erstwhile demure vulnerability. "Fergie" is a thoroughly good sort. The nation will always *like* "Fergie", whereas they will always *love* the Princess of Wales. It could have been a different story if Prince Andrew had married a cute little blonde. The Princess of Wales's coup must cause Prince Edward to ruminate somewhat over his eventual choice of bride.

Marriages may be made in Heaven but they tend to have a geographical location on earth. The key to the Wales's match was Sandringham – the world of shooting, huskies and green Wellington boots. It was fascinating to discover in King George VI's gamebook that Lady Diana Spencer's father was present when the late king shot dead his thousandth woodcock. By

Friend and confidante. Carolyn Beckwith-Smith owned the house in Clapham, South London, where Sarah Ferguson lived in the months leading up to the engagement. She was a constant support to Sarah during those difficult months, and frequently acted as a decoy for Sarah with the press.

Sarah's father and stepmother, Major and Mrs Ronald Ferguson, with their son Andrew, who will almost certainly be one of the pages at the wedding.

School group. This photograph was taken at Danes Hill School when Sarah was thirteen. She is in the middle of the back row wearing a dark jumper.

Ski-ing in style. Sarah Ferguson sports a stylish fur hat while ski-ing at Klösters with the Prince and Princess of Wales in January 1986. This was yet another indication that the romance between Andrew and Sarah was more than idle speculation. In fact, Sarah's friendship with Princess Diana was a major factor in the development of the romance with Andrew.

marrying Lady Diana, Prince Charles was veering away from the high-tech. Mountbatten era to the more relaxed country life of the Windsors.

In deathless prose Lord Patrick Beresford has extolled the virtues of the Guards Polo Club at Smith's Lawn:

'Above the stands the flags of many nations fly proudly in the breeze. In the pony lines gauchos from Argentina, seises from India and cowboys from Texas mingle with the English girl grooms, whilst out on the field an ever-flowing tide of men and horses surges backward and forward in a kaleidoscope of colour and action ....'

For the past thirty years or so Major Ronald Ferguson has been an integral feature of Smith's Lawn, risking a stray polo ball from the stick of Prince Philip and now of Prince Charles. It was at Smith's Lawn that "Fergie" and Prince Andrew became childhood friends, and no doubt to Smith's Lawn that they repaired after their Royal Ascot excursion in 1985.

They are admirably matched. They are both strong and they have both been tested. They share, we are told, the same sense of humour, emanations of which are not always totally apparent to outsiders. Whereas the last royal wedding was run as the ultimate fairy-tale romance, this one will be a glorious "whoopee" party which we shall enjoy from the wings.'

# A Princess in the Making

Some princesses are born, others are made and, for a commoner, there can be no better place to learn to be an English princess than inside Buckingham Palace. Sarah Ferguson, from the day of her engagement, had the good fortune to live there at the Queen's invitation. So in those early weeks, before she moved into Clarence House, the working girl exchanged her flat in Clapham for an apartment adjoining Prince Andrew's rooms on the second floor of the Palace, overlooking Birdcage Walk. Inevitably, in the following

A formal portrait of the princess in waiting.

Sarah and Prince Andrew join The Queen on The Balcony at Her Majesty's 60th birthday celebrations.

weeks, she imbibed some of the history and traditions of the "tied cottage" as Prince Philip once described the Royal home of some six hundred rooms.

Buckingham Palace stands on the site of a mulberry grove, planted by King James I to encourage the silk industry. The King and his advisers however, had overlooked the fact that silk worms breed exclusively on white mulberry bushes and they planted only a few of those among the common black variety. Just a handful of silk worms were produced which the King carried around in a little casket, as a sad reminder of what might have been.

Meanwhile, the failed mulberry grove became an attractive pleasure garden and an outdoor brothel where professional prostitutes claimed various secluded arbours. Samuel Pepys, the diarist, visited it for the first time on 20th May, 1668 and found it;

> "...a very silly place...and but little company, and those a rascally, whoring, roguing sort of people, only a wilderness here, that is somewhat pretty, but rude. Did not stay to drink, but walked an hour, and so away to Charing Cross..."

Two successive homes were built and pulled down in the pleasure gardens before the Duke of Buckingham built his fine Buckingham House there. Later it was bought by George III as a domestic hideaway for his beloved Queen Charlotte, conveniently close to the Royal residence, St James's Palace. He made lavish alterations there and Queen Charlotte bore him fifteen children in twenty years.

The King's debauched successor, George IV, planned to build a new palace there "to outshine the most glorious residence of any monarch in the world." Parliament disagreed so the King, under the guise of restoration, had the house demolished and replaced by a palace designed by Nash, but he died before it was completed. His successor, William IV, allowed the work to continue but with a new architect. He hated the place and died just as it was ready for occupation.

Within weeks of his death his successor, his eighteen-year-old niece, Queen Victoria, reluctantly moved into Buckingham Palace and, from 13th July, 1837 it became the official Royal residence. Less than three years later, on her wedding morning, the young Queen sent a note to her bridegroom Albert, soon after dawn, in his bedroom two corridors away.

> "Dearest," it read. "How are you today, and have you slept well? I have rested very well and feel very comfortable today. What weather! I believe, however, the rain will cease. Send one word when you, my most dearly beloved bridegroom, will be ready. Thy ever faithful, Victoria."

So nearly a century and a half later, Sarah Ferguson was setting no precedent in staying in the same home as her bridegroom before their wedding.

Buckingham Palace is alive with memories of Queen Victoria and her successors. It is a personal museum for the Queen and her family and Prince Andrew's bride could have seen the Louis XVI gilt bed in which he was born, kept in the five-roomed Belgian Suite occupied by Edward VIII during his brief uncrowned reign. The Palace is also a home, an official reception centre and a working place. There could be no better place for the future princess to

Royal dress designer Lindka Cierach.

Sequined Sarah stealing the limelight at a charity fashion show.

work through the mini-library of royal biographies, a prescribed task on her arrival, alongside her regular discussions on royal protocol with Lady Susan Hussey, the Queen's Lady-in-Waiting.

"What exactly is protocol?" a naive painter friend once asked Prince Philip.

"If you don't know you're a very lucky man," was the wry reply.

Although the Palace is a working place for the Royal family, it is never associated with commercial projects. Therefore while Sarah Ferguson intended to continue her work with a Swiss-based fine art printing and publishing company, she had to make new office arrangements. Once her engagement was official it was impossible, in view of the publicity she engendered, to continue to work at the firm's offices so the indomitable Sarah established her office at a secret address nearby and commuted to it daily.

She had been promoted from the pre-engagement days when her job sometimes included "Hoovering the floor and making tea," and was in charge of editing several art books including a collection of architectural drawings from the private collection of her future mother-in-law. As the wife of a serving naval officer her job will help to fill the long months while Prince Andrew is away at sea.

Meanwhile, during the first month of her engagement, one of her first involvements with tradition took her to the College of Arms. Anyone entering the Royal Family should have their own heraldic identity in the shape of a coat of arms and Sarah spent two hours discussing the one she had designed with Garter King of Arms (Lieut-Col Sir Colin Cole) and Norroy and Ulster King of Arms (Mr John Brooke-Little), both acting under the authority of the Crown. The future Princess had to arrange to have a coat of arms because neither of her parents had one.

Royal Ascot: The Queen Mother chats with Prince Andrew and Sarah whilst the Queen walks ahead.

A coat of arms is an honour emanating from the Crown and is available to anyone who can show they are a "worthy and honourable person." The cost is £960 for a man and £650 for a lady. The discrepancy in price is because a man's coat of arms consists of a shield and crest – a relic of the days when he bore his shield into battle and his crest on his armour. Women did not fight and their arms appear as a lozenge or diamond-shaped shield.

The heraldic insignia prepared for Sarah Ferguson, to her own design, is untraditional and very distinctive. It shows a bumble-bee resting on a thistle with three flowers, growing out of a grassy mound, all contained in a gold lozenge. Surmounting it is a traditional three-looped pinkish-purple bow which could be interpreted as a true-love knot.

Bumble-bees and thistles have been used as a crest by many Ferguson families and perhaps Sarah liked the idea of incorporating them in her coat of arms. Alternatively, the thistle could represent the romantic link in her line of descent, to the Royal House of Stuart, or even serve as a permanent reminder that it was in Scotland that Prince Andrew proposed to her. Presumably, the bumble-bee indicates hard-working intentions.

The serrated edge to the lozenge echoes the outline of her diamond and ruby engagement ring, designed by Prince Andrew, and the motto, "From Adversity Happiness Grows", suggests past difficulties in her life, once overcome, may contribute to her future happiness.

After the marriage Sarah's coat of arms will be joined, on the right, to her husband's which is the Royal coat of arms differenced by a white label of

On behalf of The Queen, Sarah presents The Queen's Cup to the winning team, 'Les Diables Bleus'.

An intimate moment with her father at Windsor.

three points, showing he is the son of the Queen. The centre point bears his distinctive mark of a blue anchor.

Choosing a trousseau was also a top priority job and possibly a rather daunting one for a future princess who was used to buying her clothes "off the peg" and apparently was not over-preoccupied with her wardrobe.

Princess Diana could have proved a sound adviser and Sarah had several fashion-conscious girl friends. Among the designers she chose many were comparatively young and unknown, like Paul Golding, a twenty-seven-year-old Oxford graduate and architectural student who had only been in the fashion business for three years. Sarah, with supreme optimism but apparently without the Princess of Wales's sure fashion sense, confidently put herself in her designers' hands.

Golding said they were introduced by a mutual friend and, by the time of her engagement, she was visiting his Georgian terrace house, overlooking the Thames, once a week for discussions and fittings. He said he had a dummy of her figure but it made it easier for his assistants to fit her personally.

Returning brown and bubbling from a holiday in Antigua.

"Her red hair is a challenge," he said, "although red heads, particularly when they have the type of skin she has, that tans easily, can wear practically any colour they like.

"She has definite ideas but luckily we agree and she then goes on to say 'What do you think I should have?' and gives me full rein."

Presumably it was a similar procedure at the other fashion designers she visited.

One of the most experienced was fifty-three-year-old Gina Fratini who has been established for twenty-five years. Sarah ordered three ballerina-length party dresses and one long evening gown from her in the first weeks of her engagement and went for fittings to the small workroom in Fulham.

"She's great. She's wonderful and brave because she can wear anything," was the verdict of this talented designer of romantic clothes who works with a team of five.

Sarah's most frequent fittings for a dress however, were in the modest looking home-cum-workroom of the designer *The Tatler* described as "The Hottest Society Dressmaker" but who nevertheless was virtually unknown in the London fashion world. She is South African born thirty-four-year-old Linda Cierach, the daughter of a Polish war hero and an English mother. Sarah ensured the world would soon know about her by inviting her to make her wedding dress.

Linda started dress-making in her sister's flat eight years ago after studying at the London College of Fashion for two years. Afterwards she worked for a short time as assistant designer with a Japanese couturier in London and Paris. Her clients included the Duchess of Kent, the exiled Queen of Greece and Sarah's former flat mate, Caroline Beckwith-Smith whose wedding dress she made. She has a reputation for calm cheerfulness and she feels it is vital to be able to see what really suits a customer's personality;

"I want them to feel as I do when I'm at my best; confident, sensuous, fun and attractive," she said.

Sarah Ferguson, as a bride and princess, gave this designer her biggest opportunity.

Sightseeing in Antigua with old schoolfriend Florence Belmondo.

Meanwhile, Sarah wore two of Paul Golding's designs at Ascot, matched to easy-to-wear hats, the hall-mark of the experienced milliner Jane Smith who has designed all Laura Ashley hats for the past fifteen years. She and Sarah had no need to meet each other.

"Paul passes on to me the measurements and shapes of the hats to be worn with his designs and suggests materials and I make up simple shapes. It's the way they're worn that matters. That makes them," she said.

Sarah found her other milliners were not as accommodating and wanted at least one fitting.

The press voted two of Sarah's Ascot outfits "disasters" and the *Daily Express* quoted Paul Golding as saying

"Please be kind to me."

It also reported that "Fergie was blissfully happy and completely unaware of the stir her outfit was causing – once again demonstrating she couldn't give tuppence for the rules of the rag trade... Loser the dress may be, but smiling Fergie won the day." Sarah was perhaps recalling that it was at Ascot, exactly a year ago, that her romance with Andrew really started. Nobody commented on her outfits in those days.

Lost in a sea of "fergie" daffodils.

Prince Andrew and Sarah arrive at The Pavilion Theatre in Weymouth for a gala night in aid of King George's Fund for Sailors.

Taking tips on Royal walkabouts from Princess Margaret at The Chelsea Flower Show.

Nevertheless, one of the hardest parts of learning to be a princess must be to school oneself to ignore press criticism completely or, otherwise, to accept the grain of truth that might well lie behind embarrassingly outspoken comments and not feel acutely self-conscious at the next public appearance.

Again Princess Diana or "B.F." as Sarah is reported to call her Best Friend, was on hand to give some hard-earned advice. It was early days to follow what has been described as the Buckingham Palace policy; "Don't read anything they write about you and take no notice of anything they say."

The newspapers had plenty to say and found plenty of people ready to give their opinions;

"If only she would lose weight and style her hair;" pleaded the American dress designer, Bill Travilla in the *Daily Express* and went on to advise Sarah to loose ten to twelve pounds in weight.

She did change her hair style;

"In two months they've turned her from a girl with flowing glossy hair and a windblown charm into a sturdy frump," was a press comment made when she appeared with her hair drawn back into "one of those dreadful bows."

A different hair style produced a similar comment from *The Star* when Sarah was photographed with Prince Andrew for the cover of the Royal Wedding Official Souvenir with her hair unswept.

"They've finally succeeded in turning fun girl Sarah Ferguson into a frump," she could have read.

The future Princess made no secret of trying to loose weight. Her daily work-out at a Mayfair Health Club stopped after her engagement but she could still have private sessions at Buckingham Palace and a daily swim in the pool there.

Photographs showed she had obviously shed a few pounds in weight on a week's holiday with a school friend, Florence Belmondo on the Caribbean island paradise of Antigua, in the luxury villa of Florence's father, the French actor Jean Paul Belmondo. The villa is set in five acres of grounds and Sarah flew there in early June under the name of Miss L. Watson. There she relaxed and swam and sunbathed in secluded coves and went for picnics in the family speed boat, *Bullit*, always accompanied by a police bodyguard and a gentleman from the Belmondo estate.

The press there were on the alert and, again, Sarah was disarmingly approachable, perhaps presaging a new royal style in media relations. She was dining one evening in a party of four at the Admiral's Inn, an eighteenth century restaurant, when she recognised two journalists at the next table.

"Isn't this a delightful place?" she said. "I hope you enjoy your meal."
A few minutes later she sent a waiter to their table with a bowl of lilies.

"I'm sorry I can't make it champagne," she said when they thanked her.
But the journalists could and they sent a bottle of champagne over to Sarah's table.
She raised her glass to them.

"Enjoy your holiday," she said and when she and her party left the restaurant she sent the remainder of the champagne over to the donors, explaining she would like them to have some too. Later a message was given to them to say Sarah had thoroughly enjoyed the meal and appreciated the way the journalists had handled it, so that there was no problem at all.

When one of the two reporters described the encounter in the *Daily Mirror* his article concluded;

"She is at peace with the world and has an extremely good relationship with Fleet Street. *We like her and she likes us.*"

Back from her week's holiday Sarah fulfilled her first official public engagement with Prince Andrew. It was a Royal Gala naval charity performance at the Pavilion Theatre, Weymouth and, appropriately, had been organised by the local committee at the Portland Naval Base where the Prince had trained as a helicopter pilot.

Sarah's holiday tan was shown to advantage by her low necked turquoise taffeta dress with a ruffled collar, full-skirted and tight-waisted. The Prince had just finished his officer's course at the Royal Naval College, Greenwich and wore a dinner jacket. His next posting was to H.M.S. Osprey Naval Air Station at Portland to fly with 815 Naval Air Squadron.

The next day the couple were at Windsor for a Sunday afternoon polo match where Sarah presented the prizes, including the Queen's Cup. Whether by accident or design, she and Princess Diana both promoted a current fashion trend by wearing complimentary spotted outfits. Sarah wore a white dress with black spots while her future sister-in-law sported white with red spots. They made an impressive pair.

Sarah had chosen to wear another spotted dress – bright green silk with black trim – for her first Royal walkabout when she went to the Chelsea Flower Show with the Queen Mother and Princess Anne. Public interest was focused on a striking daffodil, appropriately named "Fergie" and there was a rush to buy the bulbs at £10 each, to commemmorate the Royal Wedding Year. Few people appreciated that the name was a pure coincidence for the grower had registered it four years previously and had called it after a friend's son. However, his description in the catalogue was appropriate to the better-known Fergie;

"Circle of golden petals almost lost behind the largest bowl of flaming orange red that I have seen in a daffodil."

There was a surprise visit to Northern Ireland with Prince Andrew where Sarah showed typical Royal courage and unconcern for potential danger. Police security men and SAS marksmen were on guard wherever she looked but she laughed and joked her way through the crowds and chatted with patients after she and Andrew had opened the Belfast City Hospital's new tower block. The couple then drove in an open car to Hillsborough Castle for a garden party for the families of the Northern Ireland police. There Sarah planted her first tree. They also attended the Royal Ulster Constabulary's sports day. The RAF had flown them in and the Royal Navy took them home.

In between public appearances, behind the scenes, Sarah was kept busy attending to the guest lists for the wedding and the dinner given by her father the night before, posing for official photographs, discussing the wedding arrangements at Westminster Abbey and attending a rehearsal there and, like many brides, coping with wedding presents, but on a very grand scale.

Anyone requesting permission to send a gift was asked to make a donation instead, to the King George's Jubilee Trust, devoted to young cripples and children suffering from fatal diseases.

For those invited to the wedding however there were wedding lists with suggestions at several London shops. At the end of April Sarah, accompanied by a detective, spent two hours at the General Trading Company in Sloane Street, choosing some five hundred items she and Andrew would like to have. They ranged from a Dartington glass vase at £3.95 to a Georgian dining table with five leaves and eight reproduction chairs which cost £5,496. The seats of the chairs were covered in calico so that they could be re-covered to match the colour scheme of Sarah's dining room.

In between the two price extremes were three dinner services, one of Coalport fine bone china with a navy border. One plate cost £23.30 but there were two slightly cheaper services by the Hungarian manufacturers, Herend. There was also a beautiful breakfast service in Ginori's fruit design. Two pairs of antique Chinese vases, a leather photograph album, a cachepot and a brass fender were on the list along with a nineteenth century coal scuttle and a set of moulded plastic garden chairs with grey and white striped cushions.

The outdoor life which Sarah and Prince Andrew obviously intend to lead

Sharing a joke at the races – Major Ferguson is still laughing even after being "crowned" by a polo mallet.

was catered for at Asprey's in Bond Street where the wedding list started with gifts at £10 and included two picnic rugs and a large and a small shooting stick.

Sarah enjoying a nautical outing with her sailor Prince on an open boat during their visit to Northern Ireland

The higher price range included clocks: a grandfather clock at £16,000, carriage clocks at £2,800 and £1,900 and a rosewood bracket clock at £14,895. There was also a cabin trunk, a writing case and a desk set, swizzle-sticks and an electric pepper mill, a mahogany card table at £7,250, ashtrays, a visitors book and an unexpected choice of a gentleman's black fountain pen which cost £138.

The insight into the royal couple's future life-style continued at Eximius in Walton Street where Sarah had chosen, "lots and lots of photograph frames." They were in wood, leather or moiré silk. There were also red or green wood cachepots, trays, an ice-bucket and decanters.

When Sarah found she had a day to spare from all her obligations, she chose to spend it by tackling the driving course at the police training centre at Hendon, North London and learnt to handle a modified police Rover in difficult situations such as steering out of dangerous skids on the wet skid pad. Her instructor's verdict was:

"She's a very good driver and coped very well."

The indications are that this Princess in the Making will always cope very well in the variety of situations in which she will find herself. Prince Philip, endorsed that prophecy in a magazine article about himself and his family;

"I think that Sarah will be a great asset," he said.

# Previous Royal Weddings

The marriage of Queen Victoria and Prince Albert of Saxe-Coburg at the Chapel Royal, St. James's in February 1840. The young Queen gazes adoringly at her bridegroom as she plights her troth, watched by her uncle the Duke of Sussex (in skull-cap), her mother the Duchess of Kent (on right, facing), the Dowager Queen Adelaide and "Uncle Leopold", the King of the Belgians. The little girl to the left of the picture is Princess Mary Adelaide, later Duchess of Teck and the mother of Queen Mary.

The splendour and pageantry surrounding Royal weddings today were unknown until the early part of this century. Before then Royal marriages were private family affairs. But there was nothing private about the wedding night itself because it was the custom for the court to see the Royal couple as they lay in bed together for the first time after their marriage. This happened until King George III married Princess Charlotte of Mecklenburg-Strelitz in 1761.

The young King had proposed to his bride by proxy and her journey to

England, immediately afterwards, had proved extremely onerous. The Royal yacht had battled with North Sea gales for a fortnight and the Princess was the only passenger who was not sea-sick. She never missed a meal and played her harpsichord, hoping to cheer the sufferers with her music.

The yacht was forced to land at Harwich instead of at Greenwich where a Royal welcome had been prepared. The Princess was hurried to London and, arriving at 2.30 p.m. on 8th September, was told her wedding would take place that night. She promptly fainted. She recovered to meet her groom for the first time at St James's Palace where they were married in the Chapel Royal at 9.00 p.m. Afterwards, it was found that the kitchens had failed to prepare the marriage breakfast.

The bride again entertained on her harpsichord while the mistake was rectified but it was so late when the company sat down to eat that immediately afterwards the exhausted guests went home to bed. The Royal bridal couple were left alone and a long-standing Royal marriage custom was waived forever.

A guest at the wedding, Horace Walpole, noted that the Queen's ermine-lined violet-coloured mantle dragged itself and almost all her other clothes nearly halfway down her waist. Beneath it was a silver and white gown and it fastened on her shoulder with a bunch of large pearls. The spectators, Walpole commented, therefore knew as much of her upper half as the King would himself.

The eldest son of that marriage, George, Prince of Wales (later King George IV), married in 1795 also in the Chapel Royal at St James's. His was an arranged marriage and when George first saw his physically unattractive bride, Caroline of Brunswick, he swore vociferously, shouted to a footman to fetch him a glass of brandy and spent his wedding night prostrate in the hearth in a drunken stupor. He separated from his wife immediately after their daughter Charlotte was born.

Princess Charlotte, heiress presumptive to the throne, had an unhappy and disturbed childhood and grew into a beautiful but rebellious young lady. In 1813 her father tried to marry her to Prince William of Orange but she refused and fell in love with the fortune-seeking Prince Leopold of Saxe-Coburg. They met while he was in London with the Allied Sovereigns to celebrate the victory over the French.

At their marriage, at Carlton House on 2nd May, 1816, the fair-haired bride wore a dress of silver, Brussels lace and white satin that shimmered in the light of a thousand candles. The night before her marriage she had stayed at Buckingham House and when she descended the Grand Staircase in her bridal gown, her Aunt Princess Mary who was with her, wept profusely as if she had a foreboding.

The bride was led to the altar by William, Duke of Clarence who must have thought the marriage removed any chance he had of succeeding to the throne.

The honeymoon was spent at Oatlands, lent to the bridal couple by the Duke and Duchess of York. Eighteen months later Princess Charlotte gave birth to a dead son and died a few hours afterwards. The *accoucher*, Sir Richard Croft, blew out his brains.

So William, Duke of Clarence destined, to be King William IV, was one step nearer his throne and it was time to find a suitable bride after a twenty-year dalliance with Mrs Dorothy Jordon.

The marriage of George, Prince of Wales and Caroline of Brunswick at the Chapel Royal, St. James's on 8 April 1795. This rather artificially contrived grouping was painted by Henry Singleton (1766–1839) and is in the Royal Collection.

At fifty-two he married twenty-five-year-old Princess Adelaide of Saxe-Meiningen at a double wedding at Kew Palace on 11th July 1818. The other couple were his brother, the Duke of Kent and Princess Victoria Maria Louisa of Saxe-Coburg who had previously been married in her country according to the Lutheran rite. They took the opportunity to re-marry at Kew according to the rites of the English Church.

The weather was perfect. An altar was fitted up in Queen Charlotte's drawing room at Kew Palace and the massive plate was brought from the Chapel Royal. Both marriages were performed by the Archbishop of Canterbury assisted by the Bishop of London and the brides were both given away by the Prince Regent.

The double entry in the marriage register was witnessed by the dozen royal members of the families who were present. Then the Queen felt sick and retired to her room and the remaining party of eighteen or so enjoyed a gargantuan dinner at five o'clock, ending with "ices and fruit most choice consisting of remarkably fine melons, pines, grapes, peaches, apricots and plums." Afterwards, William and Adelaide retired to St James's Palace and the Duke and Duchess of Kent left for Claremont in Esher, formerly the home of the late Princess Charlotte.

William had already fathered ten illegitimate children but no child survived from his marriage to Princess Adelaide so that, on his death, the crown passed to his niece, the young Princess Victoria.

Twenty-year-old Queen Victoria was married in the Chapel Royal at St James's Palace on 10th February 1840, rather than in Westminster Abbey because, she said, she did not wish her marriage to be classed with her coronation. She was three months older than her bridegroom, Prince Albert of Saxe-Coburg and Gotha and was very conscious of it.

The Archbishop of Canterbury married them at noon before a tightly-packed assembly of five hundred peers and peeresses, Cabinet ministers and their wives, ambassadors and members of the Royal Household.

Crowds had collected in the street from eight in the morning to cheer the processions from Buckingham Palace, where martial music was played in the courtyard, to St James's. The bridegroom's procession was first, he pale and pensive wearing his picturesque Coburg Field Marshal's uniform with two large white satin rosettes on his shoulders. The Queen's procession followed ten minutes later.

The tiny Queen wore white satin trimmed with orange blossom and a chaplet of orange blossom on her head. Her veil of Honiton lace was arranged according to the custom of Royal brides so it did not hide her face. She wore the Collar of the Garter and a diamond necklace and earrings. Her twelve bridesmaids were in white.

One of them, Lady Wilhelmina Stanhope wrote;

"Her train was of white satin, trimmed with orange flowers but rather too short for the number of young ladies who carried it. We were all huddled together, and scrambled rather than walked along, kicking each other's heels, and treading on each other's gowns... The Queen presented each of her bridesmaids with a brooch, an eagle (Prince Albert's crest) of turquoise and pearls. After that she took her departure..."

That was after the bridal party had returned to the Palace and the guests had drifted away, for the wedding breakfast was a family affair. The cake was nine feet in circumference, weighed three hundred pounds and cost one hundred guineas.

Albert and Victoria left for Windsor at four o'clock. They travelled alone, followed by three carriages taking their courtiers. They reached Eton two-and-a-half hours later to be greeted by five thousand lights, more than five hundred boys and a sky full of rockets. The town was *en fête* with celebration dinners and free food and drink for two thousand poor, for which the Queen had contributed twenty pounds.

Victoria and Albert dined with six of their suite before retiring. Victoria had a headache, ate little and relaxed on a sofa. Later in their private apartments Albert played the piano for a while before he went to her bedside. He always turned to music in moments of stress.

Eighteen years later the first of their nine children, Victoria, Princess Royal, stood in the place where her parents had married to marry Prince Frederick William of Prussia, ten years her senior. So many people had been invited to the wedding on the 25th January, 1858 in the Chapel Royal that the organisers tried to accommodate them by allocating twenty inches for

The marriage of Albert Edward, Prince of Wales (later King Edward VII) and Princess Alexandra of Denmark in St. George's Chapel, Windsor 10 March 1863. Queen Victoria mournfully gazes down on the scene from the semi-seclusion of the "Royal Closet".
Note the proud air of the bride's mother at the left of the picture and the exotic presence of Maharaja Dhuleep Singh, an honoured guest on the occasion.

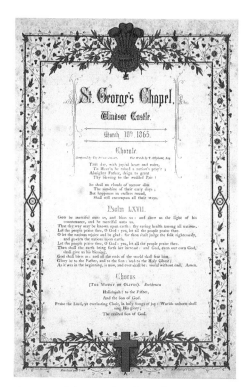

A page of the service sheet for the marriage of Albert Edward, Prince of Wales (later King Edward VII) to Princess Alexandra of Denmark in March 1863.

The menu for the wedding breakfast of Princess Beatrice of Osborne in 1885.

male backsides and twenty-four for female. They had been over optimistic and much damage was done to the ladies' costumes.

The marriage of Queen Victoria's second daughter, Princess Alice to Prince Louis of Hesse, was more like a funeral than a wedding. It had been postponed because of Prince Albert's death less than a year before and took place at Osborne, the Royal home in the Isle of Wight where the grief-stricken Queen spent much of her period of mourning.

There was a funereal air too about the wedding of Albert Edward, Prince of Wales (later King Edward VII) to Princess Alexandra of Denmark on 10th March 1863, the first Royal wedding to be held at St George's Chapel Windsor since Henry I's in 1122. Queen Victoria was still melancholy and grieving;

"I dread the whole thing awfully," she wrote. "It is for me far worse than a funeral to witness."

She dismissed the Church's protests that it fell in Lent by saying she was staging a religious ceremony and not a variety show.

One of the loveliest churches in the world, built by King Edward IV in 1478, could accommodate only nine hundred guests and the ladies lucky enough to be invited were disappointed that mourning for the Prince Consort still meant they must wear grey, lilac or mauve. Londoners were disappointed at being cheated of "a day off" to see the beautiful bride but new photographic processes ensured her photographs reached every part of the country.

Four carriage processions from Windsor Castle to the Chapel took the Royal guests, the Royal family and household, the bridegroom and the bride. The Queen went independently to the Chapel via the Deanery.

The Prince of Wales waited ten minutes at the chancel steps until his bride arrived, her long train carried by eight bridesmaids. As she entered the Chapel Jenny Lind, "the Swedish Nightingale", sang the *Chorale* for which the Prince Consort had composed the music. At the first verse his widowed Queen burst into tears.

The bride looked exquisite in a tiny-waisted satin gown, its bouffant skirt covered with silver embroidery and Honiton lace. Orange blossom ringed her brown hair. She and her bridesmaids moved so beautifully that the novelist Thackeray was reminded of a fairy-tale featuring swans.

A distraction was caused by William, the unruly son of Vicky, Crown Princess of Prussia, who removed a cairngorm from the dirk of the dagger of his Scottish outfit and hurled it across the choir. His uncle, Prince Leopold of Albany, who was similarly dressed, reprimanded him and was bitten on his bare leg for his pains.

After the ceremony, conducted by the Archbishop of Canterbury, there were three separate luncheon parties at the Castle; a large one for most of the guests, one for thirty-eight Royalties in the dining room while Queen Victoria and her youngest daughter, Beatrice, lunched alone.

Windsor Corporation spent £40,000 on decorating the streets through which the newly-weds would drive to the train for their week's honeymoon at Osborne. The crowds lining the route went wild, led by the boys of Eton who broke through police barriers and wooden palisades. One pupil, Lord Randolph Churchill, father of Sir Winston, wrote that he got to the door of the Prince's railway carriage;

"He bowed to me," he wrote, "...but I shrieked louder. I am sure, if the Princess did not possess very strong nerves, she would have been very frightened."

Windsor weddings were the fashion for the next four Royal marriages. On 5th July, 1866, at Windsor Queen Victoria's third daughter, twenty-year-old Princess Helena, married the impoverished Prince Christian of Schleswig-Holstein who, optimistically, had hoped to marry the Queen herself.

On 21st March, 1871, the bride's younger sister, Princess Louise, broke the rules by becoming the first princess to marry a commoner since 1515 when Henry VII's daughter, Princess Mary, married the Duke of Suffolk. The Germans wanted Louise to marry a Prussian prince but she had fallen in love with the Marquess of Lorne, later the 9th Duke of Argyll. "The Maiden all for Lorne", as the Princess was known, threatened to enter a convent if she was not allowed to marry her true love.

Queen Victoria gave permission and the wedding took place at Windsor on a glorious spring day. For once, the ghost of Albert was not present when the Queen gave her daughter away and looked happier than she had done for the past ten years. The highland custom of throwing a new broom after the honeymoon carriage as it drove away was added to the shower of shoes hurled after it.

The next Royal wedding at Windsor was that of Prince Arthur, Duke of Connaught, the Queen's third son, to Princess Louise Margaret of Prussia. The Queen had chosen Princess Louise Margaret to be her son's bride on the day she was born but Arthur insisted on searching Europe for an alternative as Prussian princesses were unpopular in England. In 1879, when he was twenty-nine and rather absentminded, the Prince fell out of a window of Buckingham Palace and landed on a policeman below which decided his mother his marriage should be delayed no longer. She settled on 13th March saying she did not care what the date was as long as he married Louise Margaret. Fortunately the Prince fell head over heels in love with his mother's choice.

The series of Royal marriages at Windsor continued when the Queen's fourth son, Leopold, Duke of Albany, married Princess Helen of Waldeck and Pyrmont there on 27th April, 1882. The Queen's youngest daughter, Princess Beatrice, then broke the tradition when she married Prince Henry of Battenberg in the little church of Whippingham, on the Isle of Wight, and was probably the first Sovereign's daughter to marry in a parish church.

The island was garlanded with flowers and festooned with flags and decorations on 23rd July, 1885. All accommodation was filled and the royal yachts were enlisted to cope with the overflow. The guest list was strictly limited but the local resources were so strained that the organist and choir from Windsor were warned that refreshments would be unavailable and they should eat en route.

St Mildred's Church was decorated with lilies, roses and evergreens when the Princess and her ten bridesmaids, all nieces, walked up the aisle to be married by the Archbishop of Canterbury assisted by the Dean of Westminster, the Dean of Windsor and the Rector of Whippingham. The bride's dress was similar to her mother's wedding gown and was trimmed with the same Honiton lace which was one of the Queen's most treasured possessions.

Princess Patricia of Connaught and her bridegroom driving from Westminster Abbey to Buckingham Palace after their wedding on 27 February 1919. The marriage of the immensely popular "Princess Pat" was the first royal wedding to take place at Westminster Abbey since the middle ages and was the occasion of great public rejoicing.

The groom, at the Queen's insistence, wore the white uniform of the *Gardes du Corps* which was quite overwhelming in a parish church.

The Queen gave her favourite daughter away;

> "A happier-looking couple could seldom be seen kneeling at the altar together," she wrote in her diary. "Though I stood for the ninth time near a child and for the fifth time near a daughter, at the altar, I think I never felt more deeply than I did on this occasion..."

The couple left for a two-day honeymoon at Ryde at 5 o'clock while the guests dined in two large tents at Osborne in the beautifully illuminated gardens. Later there was a firework display from the Royal yachts. Festivities continued until far into the night and included a dinner and dance for the tenants and servants.

The style of wedding, which continues today, was set after the First World War when Princess Patricia of Connaught, Prince Arthur's younger daughter, married Commander the Hon. Alexander Ramsay, son of the thirteenth Earl of Dalhousie in Westminster Abbey. It was the first royal wedding there for more than five centuries, since Richard II married Anne of Bohemia in 1382.

> "To be married at such an hour, in such a place, is a wonderful, a priceless thing," said the Archbishop of Canterbury in his address. "...The illustrious memories which belong to the most historic church in Christendom must uplift and invigorate and inspire."

The crowd outside the Abbey was unprecedented in size and in heart-warming enthusiasm. The popular, talented Princess had renounced her Royal status to become Lady Patricia Ramsay on 27th February 1919 and this was seen to represent a new spirit of national union.

Her Venetian style white wedding dress had a wide girdle of silver embroidery and, instead of carrying a bouquet, she wore a cluster of white heather and myrtle at her waist. Her silver train, embroidered with lilies, was carried by two young pages in Highland dress. Her lace veil, originally worn by Queen Charlotte, was held in place by a narrow myrtle wreath. It was a wedding gift and was valued at £2,000.

After a family luncheon at St James's Palace, where six hundred and fifty wedding gifts were on show, the couple left for a golfing honeymoon and afterwards set up home at Clarence House in London.

The wedding of "Princess Pat" at Westminster Abbey was comparatively small compared with that of Princess Mary there on 28th February 1922 to Viscount Lascelles, eldest son of the Earl and Countess of Harewood. It was the first big state pageant since the war and became a day of national rejoicing.

Banks of seats were erected inside and outside the Abbey and all through the night crowds arrived to line the route from Buckingham Palace. The crowd was densest in Trafalgar Square which was packed solid with people to see the Royal processions and escorts of mounted cavalry swing through Admiralty Arch into Whitehall. Marching in procession was a contingent of the Royal Scots of which the bride was Colonel-in-Chief, headed by their pipers.

Despite an adverse weather forecast, the morning was fine when Princess

Mary arrived at the Abbey with her father. Her gown was simply cut. It was silver cloth with an over-dress embroidered with silver thread and pearls and a satin train shot with silver. A tulle veil edged with pearls fell from her tiara of orange blossom matching the long spray of orange blossom at her waist. Her eight bridesmaids, one of whom was Lady Elizabeth Bowes-Lyon (now the Queen Mother), reflected her dress in their plainer gowns of silver cloth with veils falling from simple wreaths.

The King, who gave the bride away, wore a Field Marshal's uniform crossed by the Garter ribbon and Viscount Lascelles also wore the Garter ribbon with his military uniform for he had received the honour on his wedding day.

The new wedding service, a softer version of the old one which had been attacked for its crudity and coarseness, was used for the first time. After the ceremony and reception there was a balcony appearance at Buckingham Palace before the bridal couple left for the first part of their honeymoon at Weston Park, Lord Beresford's Shropshire seat. Afterwards, they travelled to Paris and Florence.

On their wedding day *The Times* devoted a seven column page to a list of wedding presents and their donors. They ranged from a grand powder puff and a copy of Robert Burns's poems to a magnificent set of jewellery from the King and Queen. It was of diamonds combined with sapphires, their daughter's birthstone.

The next year, on 26th April, Lady Elizabeth Bowes-Lyon walked down the aisle of Westminster Abbey again, as a bride. Her groom was Prince Albert, Duke of York (later King George VI), second son of King George V and Queen Mary and the first son of a reigning monarch to marry at Westminster since Henry III's son, Edmund Crouchback, Earl of Lancaster in 1269.

Three thousand invitations were sent out and guests were to be seated in the Abbey by ten o'clock. They included the huntsman of the Pytchley, in pink, and a contingent of Boy Scouts and boys from the industrial centres in which the Duke took a keen interest. Mr Winston Churchill arrived last — and late.

There had been controversy about whether the wedding service should be broadcast but permission was refused. The Archbishop of Canterbury feared that men in pubs might listen to it with their hats on.

Promptly at twelve minutes past eleven the state landau with an escort of four mounted police arrived at 17, Bruton Street for the bride and her father, the Earl of Strathmore who wore a scarlet uniform. At the same time the King and Queen left Buckingham Palace in the Glass Coach with Prince George (later the Duke of Kent).

Five minutes later the bridegroom left there wearing the full dress of the Royal Air Force. He was accompanied by the Prince of Wales, his "chief supporter", the Royal equivalent of a best man from the days when there was often rivalry among the King's sons as to who should succeed him. Appointment of a "chief supporter" indicated that age was the only priority. The Prince of Wales wore the uniform of a Colonel in the Welsh Guards while Prince Henry (later the Duke of Gloucester), who was also in the carriage, was in the crimson and gold of the Hussars.

Waiting in the Abbey were the Archbishops of Canterbury and York, the Bishop of London, the Dean of Westminster and the Primus of the Episcopal

Lady Elizabeth Bowes-Lyon (now HM The Queen Mother) travelling in an open carriage with the Duke of York (later King George VI) to Waterloo on the day of their wedding. 26 April 1923.

Church of Scotland who participated in the service.

The bride with her father and eight bridesmaids entered by the west door. Her simple dress was of ivory-coloured chiffon embroidered with silver thread and pearls. It had long medieval sleeves of Nottingham lace while her train, lent by the Queen, was of Point de Flandres lace mounted on tulle. Her veil of the same lace, fell from a wreath of orange blossoms. On her way to the altar she laid her bouquet of white roses of York and white heather of Scotland on the grave of the Unknown Warrior.

After the wedding H.R.H. the Duchess of York and her husband rode in a scarlet and gold coach escorted by cavalry through the cheering crowds. Troops lining the route saluted as they passed. They took a longer route to the Palace than the other guests and drove along St James's Street, Piccadilly and Constitution Hill so that more people could see them. At 1.15 p.m. they appeared on the Palace balcony.

The eight course wedding breakfast took an hour and a half and there were no speeches. In contrast, when the bride came to arrange a wedding breakfast for her daughter, Princess Elizabeth, the three course meal lasted twenty minutes.

Among small pieces of wedding cake distributed to the guests were seven which contained pure gold charms and there was great excitement to find the lucky tokens.

Eventually the newly-weds drove in an open carriage to Waterloo Station for the start of their honeymoon at Polesden Lacy, the Surrey home of the Hon. Mrs Ronald Greville. They went on to Glamis where the Duchess developed whooping cough. "So unromantic" wrote the Duke to his mother.

There was nothing unromantic about some of the thousands of wedding presents that came from all over the world. Many were returned because the donors were unknown in Court circles or not associated with societies or organisations with which the couple were concerned. A bottle of patent medicine four feet high came into that category.

The Needlemaker's Company sent a thousand needles with golden eyes; the City of Glasgow gave a clock that played a march four times daily on weekdays, while a replica of a Royal procession of 1804 marched across part of the face. On the Sabbath the clock was silent. One gift which could not be displayed was "Half a Moonlight Night" – a traditional dowry of the Lyon family. It dated from the days when a bridegroom and his friends raided and plundered on a moonlight night and half the proceeds were given to the bride.

> "Never in history...has a marriage been attended by so many witnesses... The whole nation – nay the whole Empire are the wedding guests."

So spoke the Archbishop of Canterbury at the first Royal wedding service to be broadcast. It was on 29th November, 1934 when Prince George, newly created Duke of Kent, married the beautiful Princess Marina of Greece at Westminster Abbey.

The bride, slim and elegant in a Molyneux gown of silver and white brocade with an English rose woven into its design, and wearing a dramatically-shaped diamond tiara, was a recognised fashion-leader. This was probably because of her eye for line and colour for she was a trained

Princess Elizabeth (now H.M. The Queen) and the Duke of Edinburgh photographed at Buckingham Palace after their wedding on 20 November 1947.

artist, like her father, Prince Nicholas of Greece, who had exhibited in London several times under the nom-de-plume of Nicholas Leprince.

The bride was a granddaughter of Queen Alexandra's brother, King George I of Greece. "She had not a cent," the King of England commented, but she was so charming and beautiful he did not hold it against her.

The wedding, with eight bridesmaids and a balcony appearance at Buckingham Palace, followed the pattern of the three previous royal weddings except for the Orthodox Greek wedding ceremony which was held later in the Private Chapel in Buckingham Palace.

The bridegroom's elder brother, Prince Henry, Duke of Gloucester was married a year later to Lady Alice Montagu-Douglas-Scott, third daughter of the Duke of Buccleuch. The wedding was to have been in Westminster Abbey but in October the Duke of Buccleuch died and the wedding on 6th November, took place in the Chapel at Buckingham Palace instead. The Princesses Elizabeth and Margaret were bridesmaids, "too sweet", Queen Mary said. That evening King George V wrote in his diary: "Now, all the children are married but David." Nineteen months later his first-born Edward Albert Christian George Andrew Patrick David, afterwards Edward VIII and Duke of Windsor married Mrs Wallis Simpson.

The Duke and Duchess of Windsor on their wedding day in June 1937.

The wedding took place on 3rd June, 1937, a week after the Coronation of King George VI and on the date of his late father's birthday. They married in the Château de Candé, near Tours, well removed from the French Riviera and, hopefully, offering a degree of privacy. It had been offered to them by Charles Bedaux, a French-born naturalised American who they had never met but who was very sympathetic to their cause.

So was the Rev R Anderson Jardine, Vicar of St Paul's, Darlington who wrote offering his services when it was known the Church of England would not marry a divorced person. He arrived the day before the wedding, defying the disapproval of two Bishops, the Bishop of his diocese and the Bishop of Fulham.

A handsome little salon was converted into a chapel with a carved hall chest draped with a tablecloth as an altar and a crucifix borrowed from the British Embassy in Paris. The London florist, Constance Spry, filled the château with flower arrangements as her wedding present.

It was a warm, sunny day when the little vicar married the former King of England, Emperor of India and Defender of the Faith to Mrs Simpson. The bride was given away by an old friend, Herman Rogers, and wore a simple dress of blue satin crepe with a matching hat. The best man was the Duke's former equerry, Major Edward ("Fruity") Metcalfe. There were a dozen guests and the King and the Duke of Gloucester were the only members of the royal family to send wedding presents.

The honeymoon was spent at Wasserleonburg, a magnificent manor in the Austrian Alps.

Westminster Abbey was the setting chosen for most Royal marriages in the next generation. There, on 20th Nov. 1947, Princess Elizabeth (now Queen Elizabeth II) married Lieut Philip Mountbatten, R.N., son of the late Prince Andrew of Greece and Princess Alice (Princess Alice of Battenberg). Before the wedding the sailor-prince was created a Royal Highness and Baron Greenwich, Earl of Merioneth and Duke of Edinburgh. He was also made a Knight of the Garter.

The bride's wedding ring came from the same gold nugget, mined in the

Welsh hills, as had her mother's. Her dress, made by Norman Hartnell, as were those of her eight bridesmaids, was sewn with ten thousand pearls and embroidered with emblems of the British Isles. The "something borrowed" was a diamond tiara lent by her mother.

For the first time in history the wedding of an heir to the throne was seen on television and photographers were allowed to film inside the Abbey. Another break with custom was the acceptance of all wedding presents. They came from all over the world and it was the Princess's idea to invite the donors to a reception at St James's Palace.

Princess Elizabeth rode to the Abbey, with her father, in the ornate Irish State Coach built in Ireland for the Lord Mayor of Dublin more than one hundred and forty years ago and admired and bought by Queen Victoria on her visit to that city in 1852. It weighs four tons and requires eight horses to draw it, four ridden by postillions. After the wedding the bridal couple returned to the Palace in the Glass Coach whose wide windows allowed the crowd a clearer sight of them.

Princess Margaret travelled both to and from Westminster Abbey in the Glass Coach when she married Antony Armstrong-Jones (later Earl of Snowdon) on 6th May, 1960. There was no sparkle of embroidery about her spectacular full-skirted dress made from three hundred yards of white organza. The glitter was concentrated in the diamond diadem from which fell her veil and long tulle train.

After a luncheon and balcony appearances at Buckingham Palace the bridal couple boarded the Royal yacht *Britannia* at Tower Pier. Television viewers saw the photographer-bridegroom point out his old rooms at Rotherhithe as the yacht glided past on the first part of the voyage to the Caribbean.

The next Royal wedding, that of Edward, Duke of Kent and Miss Katharine Worsley, took place in York Minster on 8th June, 1961. Two thousand guests attended the first Royal wedding there for more than six hundred years, since fifteen-year-old King Edward III married the slightly older Philippa of Hanault. Guests and television viewers saw the modern bride arrive five minutes late to start her fifty yards walk up the aisle, followed by a cluster of page boys and bridesmaids.

The sombre grey stone walls provided a magnificent setting, with banks of yellow roses mingled with ones of the white roses of York. The bride wore a gown of white silk gauze woven with iridescent thread. The material was made in France and gleamed and shone like mother-of-pearl, echoing the sparkle of her diamond diadem and diamond earrings. She carried a bouquet of white roses.

The bridegroom had received special permission from the War Office to wear the old scarlet and blue ceremonial uniform of the Royal Scots Greys, previously worn for the last time officially, after the First World War. A guard of honour from his regiment held an archway of swords over the newly weds as they left the Abbey for a reception at the bride's home, Hovingham Hall. The honeymoon was spent at Birkhall, on the Balmoral estate.

Another out-of-London Royal wedding took place at Barnwell Parish Church, Northants, near Barnwell Manor, the home of the bridegroom, Prince Richard of Gloucester (now Duke of Gloucester). He married the Danish-born Birgitte van Deurs on 8th July, 1972 and the wedding was at

Barnwell rather than at the bride's home so that the groom's ailing father, the Duke of Gloucester, could be present at the reception in his wheel chair. The best man was the bridegroom's elder brother, the bachelor Prince William of Gloucester who, one month later, was killed in an aeroplane crash.

Meanwhile, at Westminster Abbey, Princess Alexandra of Kent had married the Hon Angus Ogilvy, the second son of the twelfth Earl of Airlie, on 24th April, 1963. Two nights before their wedding the Queen gave the largest ball held in Windsor Castle for a hundred years. The two thousand guests included many foreign Royalties who were in London for the wedding.

The bride's wedding dress was of magnolia-tinted lace over white tulle and organdie and her "something borrowed" was a diamond tiara worn by her mother when she was a bride. Princess Alexandra was given away by her brother, the Duke of Kent, and attended by Princess Anne, as senior bridesmaid, four child bridesmaids and two young pages. The reception was held at St James's Palace.

Ten years later the senior bridesmaid at that wedding the Queen's only daughter, Princess Anne, also married a commoner Capt. Mark Phillips, a cavalry officer and fellow equestrian champion, in Westminster Abbey on 14th November, 1973. They had known each other for five years.

He wore the newly-designed scarlet and blue uniform of the 1st Queen's

Princess Anne and Captain Mark Phillips after their wedding on 14 November 1973 at Buckingham Palace.

Dragoon Guards. She wore a high-necked figure-hugging gown with wide, medieval sleeves and outlined in Tudor style with pearls, silver thread and sparkling embroidery. Her translucent veil fell from a delicate diamond diadem. Her bouquet included a sprig of myrtle from a bush at Windsor, said to have been planted by Queen Victoria. Her ring came from the same gold nugget as had her mother's, grandmother's and Princess Margaret's.

She broke with tradition by having only two attendants, the nine-year-olds Prince Edward, her youngest brother, and her cousin Lady Sarah Armstrong-Jones, a prim bridesmaid in a white Elizabethan-style pinafore dress.

There was no wedding march. The bride's arrival at the Abbey was signalled by a fanfare from trumpeters of the bridegroom's regiment. Choirs of the Abbey and Chapel Royal sang "Glorious Things of Thee are Spoken" as the bride progressed up the aisle.

For the first time security was very much in evidence and, during the service, detectives could be seen in the wings, the nave and peering down from the high gothic arches supporting the fan-vaulted ceiling while 1,400 police kept the Abbey and processional route under keen surveillance in case of terrorist activity.

Diversions were caused when one of the 291 horses in the procession bolted and threw its rider who was not badly hurt and when an over-enthusiastic spectator, anxious to see the pageantry, toppled and fell

A bold break with tradition: Prince Charles kissing his new bride on the balcony of Buckingham Palace.

133

into the fountain at the Victoria Memorial.

At the wedding breakfast at Buckingham Palace, as at her mother's wedding, there were only three main dishes on the menu: an egg dish followed by partridge and fruit salad with ice-cream.

Afterwards, the couple drove in an open carriage drawn by four white horses, for about a mile to the Royal Hospital. There they transferred to a car for the drive to Thatched House Lodge, Richmond Park and the start of their honeymoon.

"The place where the adventure really starts," was the Archbishop of Canterbury's description of St Paul's Cathedral in his address after the marriage of Charles, Prince of Wales and Lady Diana Spencer there on 28th July, 1981. Prince Charles's decision to break with tradition and be married there was a popular one because the long route to Wren's great masterpiece from Buckingham Palace enabled more people to watch the magnificent pageantry of the Royal processions.

The Queen with Prince Philip and members of their family were the first to drive along the flag-bedecked crowd-lined route. Then Prince Charles, in the uniform of a naval commander, drove in an open carriage with Prince Andrew, also in naval uniform, who with Prince Edward acted as their brother's supporters.

A few minutes later, the twenty-year-old bride left Clarence House in the Glass Coach, with her father, Earl Spencer. Her dress was of ivory silk taffetta and her tulle train was twenty-five feet long. Her veil was held in place by a family tiara. Her "something borrowed" was a pair of diamond and pearl earrings lent by her mother, Mrs. Shand Kydd. At St Pauls she was met by her five bridesmaids and two small pages.

Another innovation at the wedding was a moving solo given as a wedding gift by the New Zealand Maori soprano, Kiri te Kanawa who sang "Let The Bright Seraphim" from Handel's 'Samson' while the register was being signed. There was also the impromptu kiss between bride and groom on the balcony of Buckingham Palace, for all the world to see, and the fun of the honeymoon departure in an open carriage festooned with heart-shaped silver and blue balloons and a "Just Married" sign.

The honeymoon was spent at Broadlands, the home of Lord Romsey, grandson of the late Earl Mountbatten before the couple flew to Gibraltar and joined the Royal yacht *Britannia* for a Meditteranean cruise.

The Prince and Princess of Wales at St. Pauls Cathedral 28 July 1981.

# Sarah's Kinsmen

## Table of the pure female line of descent of Miss Sarah Ferguson of 19 generations of known female ancestors

| | | | |
|---|---|---|---|
| Sir Henry Hussey | = | | = ? |
| Mary Hussey | = | | = Henry Howard of Wiggenhall |
| Elizabeth Howard | = | | = Sir Henry Wentworth of Nettlestead |
| Margery Wentworth | = | before 1483 | = Sir William Waldegrave |
| Margaret Waldegrave | = | | = Sir John St. John |
| Margaret St. John | = | | = Francis Russell, 2nd Earl of Bedford |
| Lady Margaret Russell | = | 1577 | = George Clifford, 3rd Earl of Cumberland |
| Lady Anne Clifford | = | 1609 | = Richard Sackville, 3rd Earl of Dorset |
| Lady Margaret Sackville | = | 1629 | = John Tufton, 2nd Earl of Thanet |
| Lady Cecilia Tufton | = | 1667 | = Christopher Hatton, Viscount Hatton |
| Hon. Anne Hatton | = | 1685 | = Daniel Finch, 7th Earl of Winchilsea |
| Lady Mary Finch | = | 1716 | = Thomas Watson, 1st Marquess of Rockingham |
| Lady Anne Watson-Wentworth | = | 1744 | = William Fitzwilliam, 3rd Earl Fitzwilliam |
| Lady Charlotte Fitzwilliam | = | 1764 | = Thomas Dundas, 1st Baron Dundas |
| Hon Mary Dundas | = | 1806 | = Charles Fitzwilliam, 5th Earl Fitzwilliam |
| Lady Frances Laura Fitzwilliam | = | 1837 | = Rev. William Bridgeman-Simpson |
| Mary Bridgeman-Simpson | = | 1876 | = Walter Pleydell-Bouverie |
| Sybil Pleydell-Bouverie | = | 1903 | = Mervyn Wingfield, 8th Viscount Powerscourt |
| Hon Doreen Julia Wingfield | = | 1928 | = Fitzherbert Wright |
| Susan Mary Wright | = | 1956 | = Major Ronald Ivor Ferguson |

Sarah
Ferguson
(B1959)

| | | |
|---|---|---|
| 1 daughter of a Marquess | In comparison, Prince | and that of Diana, |
| 7 daughters of Earls | Andrew's female line | Princess of Wales, for 6. |
| 2 daughters of Viscounts | (through, of course, the | |
| 1 daughter of a Baron | Queen Mother) goes | |
| 4 daughters of Knights | back only 7 generations | |

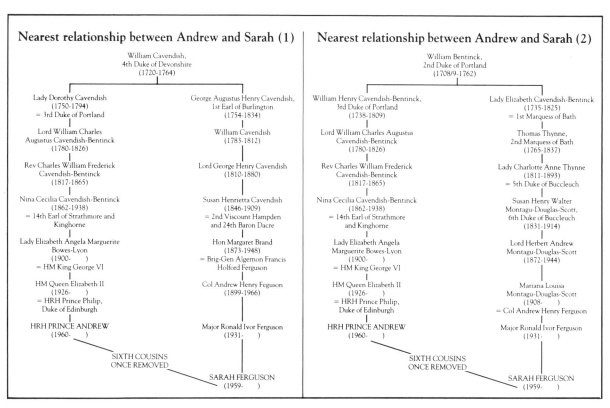

## Nearest relationship between Andrew and Sarah (1)

William Cavendish,
4th Duke of Devonshire
(1720-1764)

**Left line:**

Lady Dorothy Cavendish
(1750-1794)
= 3rd Duke of Portland

Lord William Charles
Augustus Cavendish-Bentinck
(1780-1826)

Rev Charles William Frederick
Cavendish-Bentinck
(1817-1865)

Nina Cecilia Cavendish-Bentinck
(1862-1938)
= 14th Earl of Strathmore and
Kinghorne

Lady Elizabeth Angela Marguerite
Bowes-Lyon
(1900- )
= HM King George VI

HM Queen Elizabeth II
(1926- )
= HRH Prince Philip,
Duke of Edinburgh

HRH PRINCE ANDREW
(1960- )

**Right line:**

George Augustus Henry Cavendish,
1st Earl of Burlington
(1754-1834)

William Cavendish
(1783-1812)

Lord George Henry Cavendish
(1810-1880)

Susan Henrietta Cavendish
(1846-1909)
= 2nd Viscount Hampden
and 24th Baron Dacre

Hon Margaret Brand
(1873-1948)
= Brig-Gen Algernon Francis
Holford Ferguson

Col Andrew Henry Feguson
(1899-1966)

Major Ronald Ivor Ferguson
(1931- )

SARAH FERGUSON
(1959- )

SIXTH COUSINS
ONCE REMOVED

## Nearest relationship between Andrew and Sarah (2)

William Bentinck,
2nd Duke of Portland
(1708/9-1762)

**Left line:**

William Henry Cavendish-Bentinck,
3rd Duke of Portland
(1738-1809)

Lord William Charles Augustus
Cavendish-Bentinck
(1780-1826)

Rev Charles William Frederick
Cavendish-Bentinck
(1817-1865)

Nina Cecilia Cavendish-Bentinck
(1862-1938)
= 14th Earl of Strathmore
and Kinghorne

Lady Elizabeth Angela
Marguerite Bowes-Lyon
(1900- )
= HM King George VI

HM Queen Elizabeth II
(1926- )
= HRH Prince Philip,
Duke of Edinburgh

HRH PRINCE ANDREW
(1960- )

**Right line:**

Lady Elizabeth Cavendish-Bentinck
(1735-1825)
= 1st Marquess of Bath

Thomas Thynne,
2nd Marquess of Bath
(1765-1837)

Lady Charlotte Anne Thynne
(1811-1893)
= 5th Duke of Buccleuch

Susan Henry Walter
Montagu-Douglas-Scott,
6th Duke of Buccleuch
(1831-1914)

Lord Herbert Andrew
Montagu-Douglas-Scott
(1872-1944)

Mariana Louisa
Montagu-Douglas-Scott
(1908- )
= Col Andrew Henry Ferguson

Major Ronald Ivor Ferguson
(1931- )

SARAH FERGUSON
(1959- )

SIXTH COUSINS
ONCE REMOVED

Prince Andrew and Sarah Ferguson in the Blue Drawing Room at Buckingham Palace.

# The Wedding Day

Some of the luckier spectators with a bird's eye view of the guests arriving at Westminster Abbey.

Almost five years to the day after Lady Diana Spencer became the Princess of Wales, the following announcement made at 8am on Wednesday 23rd July 1986 prevented Sarah Ferguson from being known only as Princess Andrew.

'The Queen has been pleased to direct that The Prince Andrew should be created Duke of York, Earl of Inverness and Baron Killyleagh. This will be Gazetted at 10 o'clock this morning and takes effect immediately.'

The last Duke and Duchess of York were the late King George VI and the Queen Mother, Andrew's grandmother with whom Sarah has a great affinity. She had, in fact, spent the night before her wedding at Clarence House, the Queen Mother's home.

'It will be the best day of my life' she had declared confidently of her wedding day.

Crowds had started to collect down the mile and a half of flag bedecked wedding route between Buckingham Palace and Westminster Abbey 48 hours before the wedding, and had camped on the pavement for those two days and nights. It was cold and wet on the night before the wedding and those who had managed to sleep were woken early by police when they began a security search along the procession route.

The cost of security was estimated at one and a half million pounds; the most expensive wedding item. Members of SAS units joined uniformed police and plain clothes men on the wedding route where specially-trained marksmen were on duty on the roof tops. The whole area had been combed for explosives by Scotland Yard's anti-terrorist squad working with sniffer dogs.

By 6am on the wedding morning the crowd were three rows deep in parts. By 10am they had trebled. Many were young people – contemporaries of the bridal couple and for them it was a fun occasion. The bride had said she wanted the whole nation to have fun and she intended to enjoy every minute of her wedding day. Certainly those along the freshly-sanded route took her at her word.

For some older spectators it was perhaps a sentimental occasion. Many had made long journeys because, in an indefinable way, they felt that the Royal Family was an extension of their own family and this second son, a

Prince Andrew, the Duke of York leaving Buckingham Palace with his supporter Prince Edward in the 1902 State Landau.

Prince who had chosen a commoner as his bride, had realised many people's dreams.

There was much to entertain the good-natured, friendly crowds who ignored an early shower of rain. Troops in scarlet uniforms marched to their appointed positions to line the route some six paces apart, interspersed with policemen facing the crowd. Foot guards, impressive in their scarlet tunics and bearskins, lined the half a mile of ruler-straight Mall from Buckingham Palace to Admiralty Arch. They were the Coldstream Guards, established in 1659, the Grenadiers and the Scots Guards established in 1660, the Irish Guards from 1900 and the Welsh Guards, established comparatively recently in 1915.

Down Whitehall the route was lined by the RAF and the Cheshire Regiment in their blue and white uniforms with traditional oak leaves in their caps because they were in the presence of Royalty. Nearing the Abbey, as a tribute to Prince Andrew's naval career, the Royal Navy took over and seamen and senior ratings from ships in which Prince Andrew had served were in Broad Sanctuary and formed the Path Lining party.

The Great Abbey, consecrated by Edward the Confessor in 1066 and rebuilt by Henry III, belongs, in fact, to the Queen: it is a 'Royal peculiar', independent of all bishops, and recognizes the Sovereign as its only earthly superior. The Archbishop of Canterbury, Dr. Runcie, officiates there by invitation and not by right.

Down the centuries it has been the scene of Royal funerals, coronations and, more recently, weddings, although a few medieval marriages were held there. For weeks it had been preparing for the latest Royal event in its long history.

Throughout July electricians had installed television lights in the triforium, and carpenters had erected rostra for 170 press seats, cameras and photographers. The nave was closed eight days before the wedding and the precincts five days later so that everything could be co-ordinated.

During the two days before the wedding the Abbey was decorated with

Princess Anne and Captain Mark Phillips (who were accompanied by The Earl of Westmoreland) on their way to Westminster Abbey.

masses of cream, pink and white roses, lilies and carnations blended with sprays of white gypsophila; one hundred arrangements made by forty ladies chosen by ballot from the ten thousand members of the National Association of Flower Arrangement Societies of Great Britain who worked to a colour scheme designed by their National Chairman, Mrs. Pam McNicol.

Twenty thousand blooms had been supplied by Covent Garden growers, the Royal parks and the gardens of Windsor Castle. They would be on show to the public, together with replicas of the bridal bouquets, for the three days after the wedding.

Crowds lining the route were not the only ones involved who had little sleep. At 3am on the wedding day, in the Royal Mews, gleaming horses were groomed and saddled up. An hour later four florists, led by 53-year-old Mrs. Doris Welham, were making the bridal bouquets. As a young apprentice Mrs. Welham had helped to make the Queen's bouquet of white orchids — flowers that became a Royal bridal tradition started by the future Queen Mary at her wedding. By tradition too the bridal bouquet is a gift from the Worshipful Company of Gardeners under a charter granted by King James I in 1605.

The bouquet, the garlands for the bridesmaids' hair and the flower-decorated little wooden hoops they carried had been designed by Jane Packer. She had made a garland of Lilies of the Valley and blue Muscari for Sarah to wear for the Queen's 60th birthday gala concert and, as a result, Sarah had invited her to design her wedding bouquet.

Soon after 6am Clarence House became a scene of intense activity. Sarah's team of beauticians arrived. They included her manicurist, 27-year-old Beverly Nathan, a freelance make-up artist, 35-year-old Teresa Fairminder who works for many glossy magazines, and the Scottish hairdresser, 28-year-old Denise MacAdam from Michaeljohn to wash and blow-dry Sarah's hair. She would stay to arrange Sarah's veil and head-dress after Lindka Cierach had made any last minute adjustments to the wedding gown which had been smuggled into Clarence House in the utmost secrecy. Lindka

The Prince and Princess of Wales leaving Buckingham Palace for Westminster Abbey; no doubt remembering their own wedding day five years ago.

and Denise would then leave for the Abbey ready to make any last minute adjustments to the dress, veil and head-dress in the vestry and from there to Buckingham Palace for the official photographs.

At 9am the first guests began to arrive at the Abbey to be shown to their seats by one of the hundred ushers on duty – friends of the bride and groom supplemented by thirty of the Abbey's team of forty-five honorary stewards. The men were distinctive in their special morning coats, the ladies in black velvet suits worn with lace jabots. The Abbey's honorary stewards include a formal matron of Westminster Hospital, a retired Brigadier, a chiropodist and three former Lord Mayors of London.

Among Prince Andrew's friends acting as ushers was Commander Rory McLean who served with him on the warship *Brazen* and was a victim of one of his practical jokes. Prince Andrew told him the Prince of Wales was to pay an official visit to the ship, whereupon McLean, then a young Lieutenant, had the decks swabbed and the frigate given a fresh coat of paint, only to find it was a pure hoax. Prince Andrew added to his indignity by presenting him with a 'bite trophy' in front of the crew as a mark of his gullibility.

It is the bride's prerogative to choose the wedding music and Sarah's choice, after consultation with Andrew, was 'very imaginative, ... slightly out of the ordinary and yet, at the same time, very popular' according to the Abbey organist, Simon Preston. Guests took their places to the organ music of *Allegro in D* by John Stanley, Handel's *Music for the Royal Fireworks*,

The bride leaving Clarence House with her father, Major Ronald Ferguson in the Glass Coach. This was the first glance of that famous wedding dress.

Purcell's *Trumpet Tune and Air*, Bach's *Fantasia in G* and *Air from the Suite in D*, and Handel's *Water Music*.

The family aspect of the wedding was reflected in the fact that the 1700 guests included only a few governor generals, high commissioners and government representatives. Any foreign royalty were members of the bridegroom's family.

Early arrivals at the Abbey included Lord Hailsham, the Lord Chancellor, Sir Rex Hunt, who was Governor of the Falkland Islands when Prince Andrew served there, David Steel, joint leader of the SDP/Liberal Alliance who wore a kilt, and singer Elton John in pink-rimmed spectacles. Michael Caine was there and Jackie Stewart and the comedienne Pamela Stephenson who, earlier in the week had masqueraded as a policewoman with Sarah Ferguson and the Princess of Wales in an attempt to gatecrash Prince Andrew's stag party.

Celebrities, friends and members of the family mingled in an easy informality. Mrs. Thatcher in a blue and fuscia print dress, Queen Ann-Marie of Greece in cyclamen, Mrs. Nancy Reagan in pale green silk and the bride's mother Mrs. Hector Barrantes in a golden-yellow silk coat dress and organza hat matching the flower in her husband's buttonhole.

Outside Buckingham Palace the first sign to the crowds that events were really underway came at three minutes to eleven when the Guard of Honour of the Irish Guards gave a Royal salute and, to the strains of the National

141

Anthem played by the band in the Palace foreground, the Queen's procession swung through the gates accompanied by a Sovereign's Escort of the Household Cavalry, ninety-eight strong. The Life Guards, or Household Cavalry, of which the Queen is Colonel-in-Chief date from the Restoration when they were formed to protect the Sovereign.

The Queen and the Duke of Edinburgh drove in the blue-lined Semi-State Landau drawn by four grey horses. The Queen wore a dress of delphinium blue with a wide matching hat trimmed with two blue organza peonies, a double string of pearls and pearl stud earrings. The Duke was in the uniform of an Admiral of the Fleet.

Blue was the predominating theme for the Royal ladies. Queen Elizabeth The Queen Mother and the Princess Margaret, Countess of Snowdon, rode in the second carriage in the Queen's procession, with Viscount Linley and Lady Sarah Armstrong-Jones and both wore blue. In the third carriage the Princess of Wales's turquoise and black polka dot dress matched her fine straw hat, which was turquoise on top and black underneath its sweeping rippled brim. The Prince of Wales was in the uniform of a Royal Naval Commander.

The Princess Anne and Captain Mark Phillips, were the only Royal dress dissenters. She wore a bright yellow outfit and he was in military uniform.

As the Queen's procession passed along the Mall there was a second Royal salute. To the first six bars of the National Anthem, Prince Andrew and his brother, twenty-two-year-old Prince Edward, his supporter, drove through the forecourt and out into the Mall in the open 1902 State Landau drawn by four Windsor greys. They were accompanied by a thirty-strong Captain's Escort. Few suspected that one of the two uniformed postillions riding on the carriage was a policeman in disguise.

The harnesses jingled, the sun shone and the crowd cheered as the smiling brothers waved happily and confidently. Prince Andrew wore the ceremonial dress of a Naval Lieutenant, decorated with the Jubilee Medal and the South Atlantic Campaign Medal, while the Cross of Commander of the Royal Victorian Order hung from a neck-ribbon. Prince Edward was in the uniform of a Royal Marine Officer.

The bride and her father, Major Ronald Ferguson arriving at Westminster Abbey in the Glass Coach.

The bridesmaids and page boys arrive at Westminster Abbey.

142

The strains of the National Anthem wafted back from the Queen's procession, Prince Andrew's procession was close behind and it was appropriate for the sailor-bridegroom to drive through the centre gateway of Admiralty Arch which is a memorial to Queen Victoria. The first person to drive through it was another royal sailor, King George V, the groom's great-grandfather, on his way to his coronation.

The Queen's procession had, by then, arrived at Westminster Abbey to be greeted by a special fanfare by fourteen trumpeters of Her Majesty's Royal Marine School of Music, resplendent in their red and gold trimmed blue uniforms and white pith helmets. The fanfare had been composed by the Abbey organist, Simon Preston.

Meanwhile the attention of an estimated 500 million radio listeners and television viewers swung back to Clarence House from where, at 11.15am, the elegant Glass Coach carrying the Bride and her father, Major Ronald Ferguson, drove out with an escort of six Life Guards. There was a tantalising glimpse of the bride in a head-dress of yellow and white flowers. Her fine beaded veil was scalloped with embroidered hearts and punctuated by tiny bows. There was a scooped pearl-edged neckline to her ivory satin wedding gown. For the last time in her life she was entitled to no royal honours and the bands played popular tunes such as *Get Me to the Church on Time* as she drove by.

Her small procession closely followed her bridegroom's through Admiralty Arch, past Nelson's Column in Trafalgar Square, down Whitehall and round Parliament Square to the Great West Door of the Abbey while the cheers of the crowd mingled with the joyful peel of bells from nearby St. Margaret's, the Parish Church of the House of Commons.

The world had the first full view of her wedding dress as she stepped from the glass coach and walked into the Abbey. 'There will never be another dress like it' she had said. The moment it was revealed outside the Abbey, suddenly this was an exciting wedding full of heart-warming originality.

The rich ivory silk boned bodice and full elbow-length sleeves were embroidered with bees and thistles, symbols from Sarah's coat of arms, and

Last minute adjustments to the wedding dress being made by the designer Lindka Cierach and her assistant.

The bride and her father, followed by the bridesmaids and page boys progress up the aisle through the gilded screen and into the choir amidst all the splendour of the Abbey.

bows tied with an 'S' for Sarah – all scattered with pearls. The skirt, its fullness swept to the back, was caught there in a fan-shaped bow from which flowed 17 feet of satin train also embroidered with bees and thistles with anchors, hearts and waves. The design increased in scale to the end of the train where it was surmounted with a heraldic 'A' and 'S' motif. Sarah's satin shoes were also beaded with bees and ribbons and sprinkled with pearl bugles and diamonds.

She stood, looking every inch a picture-book bride, her long titian hair arranged in a myriad of loose ringlets, a diamond and pearl pendant at her throat, falling from a pearl necklace and matching her pearl and diamond earstuds. In one hand she held a delicate fall of cream roses, gardenias, clusters of lily petals and Lilies of the Valley, matching her head-dress, her other hand clasped her father's arm.

This was a bride who loves children and her attendants were all under eight. They filed solemnly behind her in pairs, the bridesmaids wearing ballet-length dresses of soft peach slub taffeta trimmed with ecru and peach cotton lace, carrying flower-entwined wooden hoops and with garlands in their hair which matched the bride's. Paired with them were four sailors, the two youngest, 4-year-old Prince William and 5-year-old Seamus Makim, Sarah's nephew, in white sailor suits with bell-bottomed trousers and beribboned Panama hats, as worn by the young Prince Albert (later King Edward VII) in 1864. They carried seamen's small knives at their belts.

The senior page, 8-year-old Peter Philips, Princess Anne's son, and 7-year-old Andrew Ferguson, Sarah's half-brother, wore midshipmen's uniforms of the late 18th century with white knee-breeches, gilt-buttoned blue cloth dress coats with white lace jabots above their white waistcoats. They were appropriate attendants for a sailor's bride.

The chief bridesmaid was 7-year-old Lady Rosanagh Innes-Ker, eldest child of the Duke and Duchess of Roxburghe at whose Scottish home, Floors Castle, Prince Andrew proposed to Sarah. She was last in line, walking behind 6-year-old Laura Fellowes whose father is the Queen's Deputy

The Royal Family watch nervously as the bride and her father approach the altar.

Prince Andrew, the Duke of York and Sarah Ferguson just before their marriage was pronounced by the Archbishop of Canterbury, Dr. Robert Runcie, and she became the Duchess of York.

Private Secretary and whose mother was a bridesmaid at the Duke of Kent's wedding in 1961. Then came 5-year-old Alice Ferguson, Sarah's half sister and, at the front of the line, paired with Prince William, 4-year-old Zara Philips, Princess Anne's daughter and the bridegroom's god-daughter.

A fanfare of trumpets sounded before the bride began the four minute walk with her father down the wide ribbon of blue carpet while the organ played Elgar's *Imperial March* written for Queen Victoria's Diamond Jubilee. Her long train trailed gracefully behind her followed by the eight solemn little pages and bridesmaids.

The procession was preceded by clergy bearing the Cross of Westminster and as it approached Blore's nineteenth century gilded choir screen, it passed over unseen floor tablets in memory of Churchill and Livingstone. It passed through the screen's open gates and between rows of 150 official, diplomatic and governmental guests who had replaced the choristers singing from the organ loft.

The procession continued past the central lantern transcripts, to five steps rising to the sanctuary before the High Altar. At the foot of the steps Prince Andrew and Prince Edward, the tallest of the three brothers, were waiting.

The Royal Family, led by the Queen and the Duke of Edinburgh, sat to the right of the sanctuary opposite the Ferguson family.

Andrew and Sarah had chosen to use the 1662 version of the marriage service (rather than the 1928 version used at the wedding of Prince Charles and Lady Diana Spencer five years previously). Lady Diana had promised to 'love, honour and cherish' while Sarah, in response to Andrew's vow to 'love, cherish and worship' her, promised to 'love, honour and obey.'

'He's going to be worshipping and I'm obeying,' she had said; she said; 'I was thinking of obeying in moral terms' ... 'I will stress a point ... but let the man take the final decision.'

The wedding service, the same as two villagers might use marrying in a little country church, was conducted by the Archbishop of Canterbury, Dr Robert Runcie, assisted by the Archbishop of York, the Right Honourable

The Princess of Wales smiles sympathetically as Sarah Ferguson negotiates the final few steps up to the altar.

146

A mischevious Prince William found it hard to refrain from sharing a joke with Laura Fellowes during the wedding ceremony.

The Duke and Duchess of York take their first walk together as man and wife down the aisle of Westminster Abbey.

John Habgood, the new Dean of Westminster, the very Rev. Michael Mayne and the Precendor of Westminster, the Rev. Alan Luff. The team of interdenominational clergy taking part included the Roman Catholic Archbishop, Cardinal Hume, the Moderator of the General Assembly of the Church of Scotland, the Moderator of the Free Church Federal Council and the Chaplain of the Fleet.

Following tradition, the wedding ring was of Welsh gold from the Clogau St David's mine at Dolgellau, Merionethshire, from where gold for the Queen's and the Queen Mother's rings had come, and also those of Princess Margaret, Princess Anne and the Princess of Wales. Sarah's ring was made from a nugget presented to the Queen in 1981 by the Royal British Legion.

Andrew ceremoniously placed the ring on Sarah's finger, and she almost unobtrusively, slipped one on his.

After Dr. Runcie had pronounced them man and wife, Andrew and Sarah advanced to the High Altar to receive his private blessing. The choirs of the Abbey and Chapel Royal sang the motet 'We want for thy loving kindness, O God', composed by the Abbey's former organist, William McKie, for the Queen's wedding.

The Prince of Wales read the lesson from Ephesians 3:14. Then came most obvious choice of hymn for a sailor bridegroom, 'Lead us, heavenly Father, lead us o'er the world's tempestuous sea'.

Prayers by the assisting clergy were followed by The Anthem sung by the

Naughty Boy! Laura Fellowes tells a mischevious Prince William to behave.

Prince William does not appear to appreciate Laura Fellowe's advice and makes his feelings known.

Laura Fellowes, like Queen Victoria, is not amused, but Prince William thinks it is hilarious!

Lost for a reply, Laura Fellowes concentrates on the wedding ceremony whilst Prince William ponders his next move.

Is this how you do the Hornpipe? Laura Fellowes finds herself slightly off balance with such a handsome Prince beside her.

I think I've sat on my sailor's knife, but please don't give the game away!

Are you sure you can't stand up? It can't be that painful!

I'm going to pretend none of this is happening, but I wish I could read this upside down writing.

It's been a long day – even little Princes get tired.

The Duke and Duchess of York pass through the gilded screen in Westminster Abbey after the wedding ceremony, followed by their page boys and bridesmaids. The expression on their faces says it all; the happiness and delight at being man and wife.

choir; William Walton's 'Set me as a seal upon thine heart' which they had sung for the composer's eightieth birthday, nearly a year before his death in 1983. Then the final hymn 'Come down, O Love divine' was followed by a blessing by the Archbishop of Canterbury and The National Anthem.

The couple retired with their witnesses to sign the register in the Abbey's holiest and most brilliant shrine, the Chapel of St Edward the Confessor.

Ten minutes were allowed for signing the three registers, one Royal and two Abbey ones. Legally only two witnesses are required at a wedding but at a Royal one it is customary for every member of the Royal Family to sign.

Both smiling broadly, the Duke and Duchess of York prepare to step up into the 1902 State Landau for their journey back to Buckingham Palace, accompanied by the 1st and 2nd Divisions of the Queen's Escort.

The Duke and Duchess of York pass the Tomb of the Unknown Warrior on their way out of Westminster Abbey.

However, for the sake of expedience, only ten principal members of the family sign at the Abbey, and the others, including members of foreign Royal families, sign at the wedding reception.

During the signing Prince William chewed his hat elastic and fiddled with the sailor's knife at his belt while two sopranos sang in the organ loft. They were Felicity Lott, who sang Mozart's *Laudate Dominum*, and the American, Arleen Augur who sang *Exultate jubilate*, accompanied by an eighteenth century-like string ensemble.

Both families returned to their seats to wait for the bride and groom to return. Then came another surprise in this memorable wedding: When the new Duchess re-appeared her floral headdress had been removed to reveal a delicate diamond tiara – 'something borrowed' from a friend of the family.

Before commencing their long joyful walk down the aisle, the Duke and

Duchess of York paused before the Queen to bow and sweep a deep curtsey to a mother and mother-in-law who is also their Sovereign. Then to the music of Elgar's *Triumphal March* from *Caractacus* and William Walton's *Crown Imperial*, hands clasped together, they smiled and nodded informally to their friends, and the Duchess received her first curtsies as they walked down the aisle.

They were greeted by cheering crowds while the Abbey bells pealed out joyously, ringing out the wedding service with just a 'touch of bells', a twenty-five-minute peal called *Stedman Caters*. The tenor bell rang constantly, like a big brass drum, behind the changes.

Later in the day the ringers attempted a full peal consisting of some 5,000

An aerial view of the Duke and Duchess of York as they leave Westminster Abbey for Buckingham Palace.

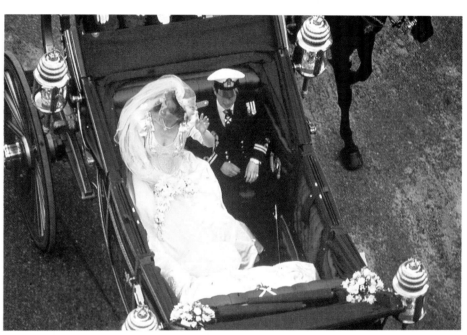

The Duchess of York steps gingerly into the 1902 State Landau, carefully arranging her 17 foot train around her.

The bridesmaids and page boys, accompanied by Prince Edward, thoroughly enjoy their trip back to Buckingham Palace, much to the delight of the crowd.

Prince Philip the Duke of Edinburgh and Mrs Hector Barrantes on their way back to Buckingham Palace after the wedding.

The Duke and Duchess of York acknowledge the cheers of the crowd.

changes lasting about three-and-a-half hours. Such peals are only rung on special occasions, mainly Royal ones, and only nineteen have been rung this century.

Smiling and waving enthusiastically to the cheering crowds, the Duke and Duchess of York drove in the open landau back to Buckingham Palace and their wedding reception. They were followed by Prince Edward in a carriage full of excited pages and two bridesmaids and another with Mrs Philip Tucker, the Ferguson nanny with four slightly less exuberant bridesmaids.

The Queen drove with Major Ferguson. His braided black tail coat had belonged to his father and was sixty-five years old but he had never needed to have it altered. He perhaps compared it with the uniforms of the Escort of

The Queen and Major Ronald Ferguson looking proud and happy after the wedding.

The Duke and Duchess of York
returning to Buckingham Palace.

The Duke and Duchess of York arriving
back at Buckingham Palace after the
wedding.

As they draw up in the 1902 State
Landau...

...Sarah extricates herself whilst over-
enthusiastic page boys and
bridesmaids...

Life Guards which he had commanded for twenty-one years and in which his
father and grandfather had also served.

The Duke of Edinburgh travelled back to the Palace with Mrs Hector
Barrantes followed by the rest of the Royal Family. They arrived just as
Prince William rushed up to kiss his Uncle Andrew and his new aunt,
whereupon all the other pages and bridesmaids followed suit.

...rush up to greet them and...

...they go into the Palace to prepare for the photographic session and balcony appearances.

Inside the Palace a comparatively unknown photographer, 43-year-old Albert Mackenzie Watson was waiting to take the official photographs. He is a Scot who lives in New York with his wife and family, works as a fashion photographer and has never photographed any of the Royal Family or, indeed, taken any wedding photographs before. Prince Andrew invited him to take the official wedding pictures after he had seen some of his work.

Like many newcomers enlisted by Andrew and Sarah, the photographer was thrilled at his big chance and said he would need to be quite firm when

The Duke and Duchess of York pretending they cannot hear the crowd shouting for what is becoming the traditional kiss.

The Duke and Duchess of York oblige with a lingering kiss.

The Duke and Duchess of York make the traditional appearance on the balcony to the delight of the crowds below.

r their second appearance on the lcony the Duke and Duchess of York rn to go back inside the Palace, but give a final wave to all their supporters below.

the Royal Family posed for him, because he wanted the wedding portraits 'to look amazing'.

It seemed most likely that some of the smaller members of the wedding party were not as co-operative as they might have been because presumably the photographic session delayed the balcony appearance. Sarah and Andrew appeared half an hour later than expected. The crowds which were packed outside Buckingham Palace and the Mall shouted for them to kiss each other. Sarah cupped her ear and pretended not to hear. But they did kiss, just once.

A five-tier wedding cake was cut at the brief wedding reception. It had been made at the Navy's catering school at Torpoint in Cornwall, stood 5

The entire wedding party appears on the balcony of Buckingham Palace.

feet 6 inches high and weighed nearly 17 stone. A duplicate cake had been sent to London in a separate van in case anything happened to the original one.

When the couple left on the first stage of their honeymoon journey she was the familiar Fergie: a laughing tousle-haired girl in a blue, green and white silk dress. They left Buckingham Palace in an open carriage and the family and members of the Royal Household pelted them with confetti and rose petals. The carriage was decorated with flags and a giant teddy bear was propped up in front of them. On the back of the carriage, family practical jokers had fixed a mock radio transmitter labelled 'Phone Home'.

A guard of honour of scarlet-coated Chelsea pensioners formed at the Royal Hospital, Chelsea, where the newly-weds took off in a red helicopter for Heathrow. From there a new jet of the Queen's Flight took them to the Azores to meet the Royal Yacht *Britannia* for a five-day cruise round the Islands.

Before they went Sarah's wedding bouquet was sent to Westminster Abbey and placed on the poppy-fringed Tomb of the Unknown Warrior.

Whereas the previous Royal Wedding, that between the Prince of Wales and Lady Diana Spencer, was, as Hugo Vickers said, 'The ultimate fairy-tale romance' this was, as he prophesied 'more like a glorious party'. And there were parties in plenty to celebrate, starting with splendid pre-wedding ones

The Duke and Duchess of York leaving Buckingham Palace for their honeymoon. They were covered in confetti and Sarah wiped a tear from her eye as she waved goodbye.

The bride and groom: The newly-married Duke and Duchess of York pose for the camera in the Throne Room of Buckingham Palace. Prince Andrew (his new title was conferred just an hour and a half before the wedding ceremony) wore the ceremonial day dress uniform of a naval lieutenant. Sarah's dress was created for her by Lindka Cierach.

given by King Constantine of Greece at Claridges, by Major Ferguson in a huge marquee on Smith's Lawn at Windsor, by Prince Charles at a Soho restaurant and by the Queen.

After the wedding, celebrations continued with a firework display at Sarah's home village of Dummer and at street parties and private parties up and down the country. Most of the Royal Family were among four hundred guests at an informal help-yourself-buffet and dance at Claridges given by Sir Geoffrey and Lady Shakerley. It was literally a delayed 'wedding breakfast', the menu consisted of the Queen's favourite kind of simple dishes, scrambled

eggs, baked beans, kidneys, mushrooms, bacon and sausages, smoked salmon, croissants, marmalade and fruit, with coffee and champagne.

Guests sat at small round tables decorated with paper daisies matching huge daisies which hung over the dance floor. The yellow daisy centres were reflected by the colour of the gowns worn by the Queen and Princess Margaret. Princess Michael of Kent was in bright pink and the Princess of Wales wore green.

The band played old-fashioned tunes like *Tea for Two* to which the Prince of Wales danced with Mrs Reagan.

Video tapes of the wedding were played all evening in rooms leading off the ballroom and among the younger guests were Marina Ogilvy, Lady Helen Windsor, Lady Sarah Armstrong-Jones and Lord Linley.

It had been a day to remember; a day when a happy, courageous, outgoing girl proved to the world the truth of Shakespeare's words:

"This above all; to thine ownself be true; and it must follow as the night the day thou canst not be then false to any man." – *Hamlet*.

**THE WEDDING DAY PICTURE CREDITS**

**COLOUR**

*Rex Features Ltd:* 1, 5, 6, 7, 137, 140, 142, 145, 146, 147, 153
*Albert Watson:* 2, 159
*Tim Graham:* 3, 8, 138, 151, 152, 153, 154, 155, 156, 157, 158
*Syndication International:* 7, 139, 142, 143, 144, 150, 155, 157, 160
*CPNA:* 7, 141, 147, 150, 151, 156
*Anwar Hussein:* 158

**BLACK AND WHITE**

*Syndication International:* 148